MINI FLASH LANGUAGE GAMES
TEACHER'S BOOK

Susan Thomas with Annie Hughes

Illustrations by Heather Clarke

COPYKIT ENGLISH

north star
ENGLISH LANGUAGE TEACHING

Mini Flashcards Language Games
Teacher's Book
By Susan Thomas
Illustrated by Heather Clarke
Additional illustrations by Steve Lillie
ELT consultant: Annie Hughes

Published by North Star ELT
5 Leverndale Court, Crookston
Glasgow G53 7SJ Scotland
United Kingdom
www.northstarelt.co.uk

Publisher: Andy Cowle
Editorial services: SunCross Media LLC
Cover design: Studio April
Text design/Composition: Christopher Hanzie
Printed by: M & A Thomson Litho Ltd.

Original work published by MLG Publishing (Miniflashcards Language Games), written by Susan Thomas, illustrated by Heather Clarke, text and illustrations copyright MLG Publishing.

ISBN: 978-1-907584-03-9

A catalogue record of this book is available from the British Library.

Contents

by Annie Hughes

- Introduction
- How we think children learn foreign languages
- Learning styles
- Mini Flashcards help create meaningful and memorable language-learning activities
- Mini Flashcards help encourage the real use of new and recycled target language
- The place of language games in teaching English to young learners
- Teacher assessment using Mini Flashcards
- Timing of games and activities using Mini Flashcards
- Language for playing games and taking part in activities

Activities & Games for Using the Mini Flashcards and Picture Pages

Topic-specific Activities and Games

Mini Flashcards Language Games

Introduction
by Susan Thomas

As learners, at any age, we make use of all our senses: sight, sound, touch, and even taste and smell. We learn in many different ways as well: by listening to what people tell us, by watching what they do, by copying them, by experimenting and finding things out for ourselves, and, above all, by practising various skills. Our learning can be passive (listening, reading, observing), it can be active (copying, experimenting, repeating), it can be individual (learning by oneself) or interactive (learning with and from others). Often it is a combination of these.

When we are learning, we find that we have strengths and weaknesses, and as a result of these we develop preferred ways of learning. Traditionally, language learning in school has emphasised aural input and text-based learning, but these are not necessarily the best or only ways for all students to learn. Awareness of the value of other modes of learning is leading teachers to attempt to broaden their approach to cater for a wider range of learning needs and preferences. Only in this way can teaching and learning become more effective.

Since 1990, together with a small group of teachers, I have been producing visual and tactile materials which help modern language teachers to provide opportunities for learning which are more multi-sensory in their appeal and which, because of their flexibility, can be used to meet a wider range of learning needs than textbooks on their own can provide.

The emphasis on games-type activities is deliberate, since the acquisition of foreign language skills is as much practical as it is academic, and it is only through frequent practice that the learner can become sufficiently familiar with the language presented to be confident enough to use it for him or herself. Constant repetition, however, can be demotivating. By incorporating new vocabulary and grammatical structures into game-based situations in which the elements appear in randomised and enjoyable combinations, learners' involvement in the learning process can be engaged more effectively and sustained for longer than is often the case with textbook exercises. Game situations, if designed with learning goals clearly in mind, can provide stimulating and challenging work which can support those with learning difficulties and promote the learning of our most gifted students.

The Mini Flashcards materials can be used to promote effective learning in the following ways. They:
- ▶ support multi-sensory approaches in language learning which are tactile, visual, and designed for active everyday use.
- ▶ can make language visible by providing visual prompts and 'manipulable' structures.
- ▶ can provide challenges appropriate for classes of all abilities and mixed abilities.
- ▶ support independent learning.
- ▶ encourage co-operative, team learning.
- ▶ help to build confidence.
- ▶ are motivating and fun.
- ▶ can be used to promote creativity.
- ▶ allow teachers to make efficient use of resources, by providing materials which are attractive, fun to use, flexible, cost effective and timesaving.

Games can be an effective way of motivating learners to practise basic vocabulary and structures to the point where they can use them confidently. Some of the games described in this book go further than this, encouraging learners to combine elements of language they have already acquired to produce new forms of the language to suit new situations. The materials supplied in this book and other Mini Flashcard packs can be used in many other ways to support the creative use of language.

Using the Mini Flashcards

The Mini Flashcards can be used to support classroom work with students of any age in a number of different ways. For example, they can:

- ▶ be used simply, as flashcards, to introduce a new word or phrase in pairwork, groups or whole class activities.
- ▶ serve as prompts or cue cards for the production of the speech in language practice activities.
- ▶ provide the starting point for introducing or recycling related vocabulary in a game or activity.
- ▶ be used to provide randomised prompts for language practice or assessment.
- ▶ be used, in their more powerful form, as the basis of an activity or game that the learners can play, engage in, enjoy and be motivated to take part in.

The Mini Flashcards are in card packs of 40 pictures (or in photocopiable form in this book) and are as follows:

- ▶ *Adjectives*
- ▶ *All About Me*
- ▶ *At Home*
- ▶ *At School*
- ▶ *Body & Health*
- ▶ *Clothes*
- ▶ *Feelings*
- ▶ *Food & Drink*
- ▶ *Happy Holidays*
- ▶ *Leisure*
- ▶ *People & Jobs*
- ▶ *Prepositions & Directions*
- ▶ *Round the Town*
- ▶ *Travel*
- ▶ *Verbs*
- ▶ *Weather & Calendar*

If you like the Mini Flashcards series, you'll love these:

978-1-907584-01-5

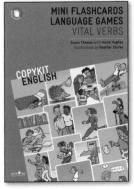

978-1-907584-04-6

978-1-907584-33-6

978-1-907584-34-3

978-1-907584-35-0

For **FREE** sample materials and more information contact **english@northstarelt.co.uk** or visit **www.northstarelt.co.uk/miniflashcards**

Using Mini Flashcards to Teach Young Learners of English

by Annie Hughes

How we think children learn foreign languages

It is very much part of life in the 21st century that more and more children, starting earlier and earlier, are learning English around the world as a foreign, additional, second or first language in school. If we are aware of how children develop, think and learn we can create the most suitable learning environment for them, which will include a range of teaching activities to enhance their language learning.

First and foremost, children learn anything, and particularly language, when they are motivated to do so. Motivation comes about for children when the content, method of teaching, focus of the activity and experience of learning and enjoyment in the teaching class are scaffolded and structured by the teacher. The teacher is central to the success in helping young learners learn English.

The language teacher needs to be aware of what the children are learning, how they are learning it, and what cognitive stage of learning they are at. The language teacher also needs to be aware of what the most suitable resources are for helping these learners use and remember the language they are interacting with and being taught, so that they will not only learn it, but will also acquire it.

One of the most successful ways of encouraging and supporting children when they are learning a target language is to use interactive, meaningful and purposeful activities in which they can use and understand the language. The Mini Flashcards and their related games reflect this approach very well. Teachers need to show their young learners how the language they are learning and using in activities is linked to their everyday lives.

Learning styles

Additionally, it is important for the teacher to address the different learning styles in the class. Howard Gardner's theory of multiple intelligences tells us that children need a variety of ways to experience learning, in order that all the different multiple intelligences which may be in the class are catered for. For example, some children learn mostly by listening, while others learn best by being physically involved in an activity. Some learn by writing things down, or drawing, while others like to watch and observe. Some children like to learn by reflecting on things, while others like to learn best by talking things through out loud. Some children learn best when their emotions are linked with an activity, while others learn best when they are being objective. Using the Mini Flashcards in a wide variety of language learning activities encourages learners to use all these different ways of learning in a natural and realistic way.

Mini Flashcards help create meaningful and memorable language-learning activities

One of the main aims of the teacher of English to young learners is to motivate the learners so that they will find the target language memorable, purposeful and fun to use in order that they acquire it. The Mini Flashcards are therefore one of the most valuable resources that can be used in the classroom. The series lends itself to many different activities that are highly motivating for young language learners, and which will cater for the different types of learners in the class.

When children enjoy and are motivated by activities and games using language, they will remember those games and want to play them over and over again. In this way, they get the target language repetition that aids language learning in a meaningful and purposeful way, Eg. they will want to win a game, or work with their partner or team to get the highest number of cards or they are simply having fun!

Mini Flashcards help encourage the real use of new and recycled target language

When a new game is played in the language learning classroom with young learners, the teacher knows that if the game has the right resources to support, scaffold and encourage language use and development, the learners will want to play and be involved, thus learning more language and consolidating their learning each time they play the game.

The Mini Flashcards are designed to encourage the real use of any topic-based language that the teacher is introducing or recycling. In this way, the games and activities that the learners are involved in will have a real purpose and have real outcomes. Often this 'winning' will be the child's motivation, while the teacher's motivation is to ensure that language is being used and remembered.

The place of language games in teaching English to young learners

Games can be an effective way of motivating learners to practise basic vocabulary and structures to the point where they can use them confidently. Some of the games described below go further than this, encouraging learners to combine elements of language they have already acquired to produce new forms of the language to fit different situations. They create an ideal medium through which young learners can recycle and develop their language, without even being aware that they are focusing so much on language. Teachers can use these language games and activities to support and supplement any course that they are following, as the cards lend themselves to use within any approach or method of teaching English.

Teacher assessment using Mini Flashcards

It is important that language teachers use a variety of assessment tools to evaluate their teaching and the learners' understanding and acquisition of the target language. Using the Mini Flashcards can make assessment of individual students or groups of students more accessible yet fun for the learners. The teacher can observe and make notes during the activities and games. Teacher assessment of individual, pair or group activity can take place:

▶ during a teacher controlled activity using the Mini Flashcards.
▶ by observing individuals, pairs or groups at work in activities and games.
▶ by joining in activities with an individual, pair or group.
▶ while observing groups to see how the language is being used within the class.
▶ by providing individuals or groups with self-assessment forms to complete, based on the visuals they are using in the activity, and perhaps adding these to learner portfolios.
▶ by using the cards as prompts to see if children understand or know English vocabulary.
▶ by observing children engaged in games which highlight the individuals' knowledge of language and vocabulary being used.
▶ by allowing the children to create games themselves for pair-work or groups, in which their knowledge of the language involved can be assessed as they create the game.
▶ by allowing the learners to show, in general, their basic interpersonal skills in the target language, including language for organising and playing language games, as well as the focus language in the actual activity itself.

Timing of games and activities using Mini Flashcards

Most verbal games will last between 5 and 15 minutes, depending on the pair, group or whole class size involved in them. However, writing games will take longer, so it is important to build in enough time for activity/game completion. Time should be allowed for setting up the activity, for class reflection of the activity or game, and to assess what has been learnt after they have been completed. During reflection, young learners can discuss what they enjoyed about the activity or game, and what language they learnt during the activity. They can feed back any difficulties they encountered and, with teacher support, what strategies they could use next time to ease these. They can help the teacher see to what extent the activity was successful, and how it might be varied or changed, amended or extended in the future to bring about a different focus or outcome.

Language for playing games and taking part in activities

Teachers will need to pre-teach games language, or language for taking part in communicative activities, so that the learners will have more opportunity to use the target language to play the game or carry out the activity. This language might include:

- ▶ *game*
- ▶ *activity*
- ▶ *pairs, groups, teams, whole class*
- ▶ *games/quiz person*
- ▶ *leader*
- ▶ *winner*
- ▶ *collect*
- ▶ *choose*
- ▶ *It's my turn (your turn, their turn, his turn, her turn)*
- ▶ *It's your go (my go, your go, their go, his/her go)*
- ▶ *You're next*
- ▶ *We win (they win, he wins, she wins)*
- ▶ *I've won!*
- ▶ *Shuffle the cards*
- ▶ *Deal the cards*
- ▶ *Pick up your cards*
- ▶ *Lay/spread out the cards*
- ▶ *Turn the cards face down, face up (picture side up/down)*
- ▶ *Put the cards in a pile*
- ▶ *Hold the cards in your hands, face down, face up, picture side up/down*
- ▶ *Mix (up) the topics/cards*
- ▶ *Don't mix (up) the topics*
- ▶ *What's your favourite?*
- ▶ *My favourite is…/My favourites are..*
- ▶ *I've got/she's got/he's got/they've got*

Activities & Games for using the Mini Flashcards and Picture Pages

The following are core activities and games that can be used with any of the Mini Flashcards in the series as well as the Picture Pages in this book. They can be used on their own or in a variety of combinations to support work at different stages of the teaching syllabus, and with students of differing ages, abilities and language levels. During any one lesson the teacher could also give different pairs or groups different language games or activities or cards, depending on their ability levels and the teaching aims.

The activities and games can be used within any part of a lesson in order to present or consolidate the language being taught at the time, or to develop, re-use or recycle previously taught language. Then, unit by unit, there are topic-specific activities and games to further develop the theme and any extra related language. There is an emphasis on speaking skills throughout.

In some activities and games you will also see that the Picture Pages can be used as full handouts or, if you haven't got the colour cards (see www.northstarelt.co.uk/miniflashcards) as Mini Flashcards which you (or your students) make by photocopying and cutting up. For some activities, you will need to make sure your colour cards have the words hidden on the back (using small labels, sticky notes, etc).

Dice & Spinners

The topics and activities can be enhanced and extended even further with dice for language, numbers, colour, tenses and mood. See page 80 a list of available dice, plus photocopiable templates to make spinners if you don't have dice, and for lots of ideas for using them with the cards or photocopied picture handouts.

1. Collect
Groups of 4
Learners spread the cards out on the desks, picture side up. The learners then take it in turns to choose a card, hold it up for all to see and try to name it. If they name it correctly, they keep the card. If they are wrong, they put the card back. When all the cards have been collected, the player with the most cards is the winner.

2. Can You Name It?
Pairwork or group work

Learners fan out some cards picture side up, for their partner or the next player in the group to choose and name. If s/he is right they win the card. If they are wrong, the card is put back into the pack. At the end of activity, the winner is the one with the most cards.

3. My Turn
Pairwork or group work

Place the cards in one pile in the middle of the table with the top card picture side up. Take it in turns to name the item on the top card. If you are wrong, the card goes to the bottom of the pack, if you are right you keep the card. The winner is the one with the most cards at the end of the game.

4. Snap
Pairwork or group work (groups of 4)

Learners are given two identical sets of topic cards. These should be well shuffled before they play. Both sets of cards should be combined and then shuffled again. All the cards should be dealt to all the learners in the pair or group. When it is a learner's turn to play, without looking at the card first, s/he takes a card from the top of their cards and puts it in a growing pile in the middle of the desk. If a card played is the same as the previous one, the first person to call out the name of the item wins all the cards in the pile. The winner is the learner with the most cards when everyone has played all their cards.

5. Guess the Card
Group work (groups of 4-6)

Place a small number of cards linked to a particular topic face down in a pile on the desk. Learners, in turn, try to say or guess what the next card is. If they are right, the card goes back at the bottom of the pile, but if they are wrong, they get the card. At the end of the game the learner with the fewest is the winner.

6. Glimpse
Group work

In a group of five, there are two teams of two and one 'games person'. The games person holds up a card for both teams to see but for one second only. The first player to name the item shown wins the card for their team. When the game is over, the team with the most cards wins.

7. Guess What's Coming
Group work. Players will need themed collections of cards in a bag, box or envelope.

In a group of five, there are two teams of two and one 'games person'. The games person starts to show the cards, and everyone should try and say what is on the card as quickly as they can. If they are correct and the first to call, they keep the card. After about 4-5 cards the games person asks 'What's coming next?' and the other players have to each guess what the next card is. The person who guesses correctly gets the card. If nobody guesses correctly the games person keeps the card. At the end of the game, see who has won - it could be one of the players or the games person. Take it in turns to be the games person.

Variation: Play this game like My Turn (above), but if you are wrong, you put the card, picture up, in front of you. At the end of the game, if you still have cards, you try again, in turn, to give the right answer and so get rid of your cards. The player with the most cards still is the loser.

8. Line Solitaire
Working alone or in pairs working together

This can be useful as an activity for learners once they have finished one activity and are waiting for their colleagues to finish. It can also be useful for learners of different abilities to play, as the teacher can sort the cards into different levels of difficulty. The learner lays out some cards in a line (these can be a mixture of topic cards or just one topic card – it's up to the teacher). The learner tries to name the first picture, then turns the card over and checks if s/he is right. If they get it right, they carry on (with the card picture side down). If they get one wrong, then they try and learn it. Then they turn all the cards back over (picture side up), and start again. The aim is for the student to get a long run of cards without any mistakes. This game could also be played in pairs, groups or teams, where the learning is a shared activity.

9. Noughts and Crosses
Pairwork. The learners will need 9 cards.
In pairs, lay out the cards (mixed topics or one topic) 3 x 3 on the table. They take it in turns to name an item. When one learner is right they turn the card over, or place a coloured counter (or piece of paper) on it. Their partner then takes a turn to name an item. If s/he is correct, the card is turned over and a different coloured counter placed on it. The winner is the first learner with three cards in a row, just like noughts and crosses.

10. I Spy . . .
Pairwork or group work. The learners will need 10 cards or more linked to one topic or mixed topics.
The learners spread the cards out over the table. They decide who is to go first and this person gives the first letter or sound of a card for the other players to find. If someone points to the correct card and names it, they keep it and become the next person to call out the letter/sound. The winner is the player with the most cards at the end.

11. Kim's Game
Pairwork or group work
Spread out some cards over the table. One player removes a card while the others look away or close their eyes. The others then look at the cards. The first player to name the missing card wins. The card is returned and the game is then played again. The last winner is then the one who removes a card, while the others look away or close their eyes.

12. Language Bingo
Group work or whole class. Choose 20 cards from a topic pack (or a handout from the 1-20 or 21-40 picture grids).
In groups, one learner should be chosen to be the games person. All those playing need to draw a grid on a plain piece of paper with 8 boxes in it. Tell the group what the topic is for the game and the 20 words involved. Then they all choose 8 words/phrases from the word list and write each of these chosen 8 into their grid boxes. From the list or by picking cards, the games person calls out the 20 cards/words in random order but keeps the cards to one side (or marks the list or pictures handout). As the games person calls out the words/phrases, the learners have to listen and cross off any words on their grid which they hear. The first learner to cross off all 8 of their words shouts 'bingo!'. This player should tell the games person which words/phrases s/he has crossed out on their grid. The games person checks that each of these has been called out and, if so, declares this player the winner and a new game can be started. The winner of the last game becomes the games person. The game can be shortened by only using 12 pictures and the learners choose 8 or even 6 words/phrases.

13. Charades
The learners should be in two teams or groups. They need a pile of cards from a specific topic or a mixture of topics.
Each team should take it in turns to do the charade/mime in order to win points. The first learner from a team takes a card from any pack without anyone else seeing what they have, and then mimes what is on the card for their team. The other team watches and also tries to guess the answer (silently or whispering to each other!). If the charade team correctly guesses the word or phrase then they get a point. If the charade team does not correctly guess the word or phrase, then the other team can guess it. If they guess correctly it then they get the point, but if not, it is then their turn for the next charade. The team with the most points at the end of the playing time is the winning team.

14. Matching Pairs
Pairwork. Students will need 2 identical sets of picture cards (all 40 or just 20 from two identical packs). You will need to make sure your cards have the words hidden on the back (using small labels, sticky notes, etc, if you are using the colour cards).
Each pair shuffles the cards and spreads them all out picture side down on the desk. The first player turns over two cards. If they match, and if the player can name them correctly, s/he keeps them and tries again. If they do not match, or if s/he cannot name them correctly, the cards are turned back down in the same place they came from and the next player tries. The winner is the learner who, at the end of the game, has the most pairs of cards.

15. I Went to Market . . .
Pairwork or group work
Spread some appropriate cards out on the table (Eg. *food, clothes*). One learner starts a sentence and the next learner repeats the sentence from memory and adds an item. If a player can't remember a word, the other(s) can help by prompting him/her with their mini flashcard.
Eg.
Learner 1: *I went to market and bought . . . a cake . . .*
Learner 2: *I went to market and bought . . . a cake and some milk . . .*
Learner 3: *I went to market and bought . . . a cake, some milk . . . and a carrot.*

You can also play it with Round the Town cards:
Learner 1: *I went to the city and I saw a church*
Learner 2: *I went to the city and I saw a church and a supermarket*
Learner 3: *I went to the city and I saw a church, a supermarket and the station*

16. Guessing Game
Pairwork or group work. You will need a set of cards related to the current topic which all the learners see before the game starts.
The first learner to play thinks of one of the cards and says something about it by describing it. The other players try to guess which one s/he is thinking of.
Eg. Happy Holidays cards: It's made of metal. You put letters and postcards in it. (Answer: *postbox*). The first one to get the right card then takes over and describes another card.

17. True or False
Pairwork, group work , or as a whole class with the teacher, or a learner, pointing to a picture and saying something about it
The other players listen carefully and look at the picture and then the first player to say/shout 'true!' or 'false!' correctly wins a point. The winner is the learner, pair or group that has won the most points.
Variation 1: As above, but the caller repeats the sentence if true, or corrects it if it is false.
Variation 2: The teacher, or a learner, reads out a list of statements. The players jot down which are true and which are false. Check all the answers at the end.

18. Definitions
Pairwork or group work
One learner takes a card and tries to define (give an explanation about) what is shown on the card. The other learners can see the card. If the definition is correct, the person who defined it keeps the card. Winners are those with the most cards at the end of play. Eg. *Café – a place where you can sit down and have a drink or something to eat.*
Variation 1: a student produces a definition with some mistakes and the next player has to correct it.
Variation 2: a student produces a definition that is completely wrong for the picture and the other students have to try to change what is wrong and give the sentence correctly. One point is given to each player who puts the wrong sentence right.

19. Only a Minute!
Group work, or as a whole class with the teacher managing
A learner is given a card, and has to talk about what is on the card for as long as possible in English. If the learner can keep going for 20 seconds they get a point, for 40 seconds they get 2, and for one minute they get 3 points. They then choose another learner to get the next card. The winner is the student with the most points, or the group with the most points between them.

20. Two's Company
Pairwork or group work. You will need a set of cards from different topics.
Shuffle the cards and then divide them into two piles on the desk. Place them face down. Each player in turn takes one card from each pile and makes up one sentence, which must combine vocabulary ideas from both cards.
Variation 1: More piles of different topics could be used, or piles could be arranged so that, for example, one pile contained people, another verbs, another objects, another joining words/phrases, and so on, and the players start to play the game with more and more cards to be used together.
Variation 2: The learners can use the cards in their pair/group to create a story to explain what is happening in the pictures.

21. Group Sentence Swap
Group work. You will need 2 sets of pictures—a different set for each group.
Each member of each group writes a sentence on a slip of paper about their pictures. These sentences, as separate sentences on separate pieces of paper, should be mixed up. The groups then swap the cards and sentences with another group. Each group then has to match the sentences with the cards. The first group to finish the matching correctly wins.

22. Storyboard
This activity can be done in groups of four, and you will need cards of mixed topics. Allow plenty of time for this activity, or allow the learners to take part in it over more than one lesson.
Each learner in the group gets 3 cards from the top of a pack of cards. Each player then writes down a short story using vocabulary/ideas from all the cards. Each player then tells/reads out their story.
Variation 1: in groups of 3: each learner has one card each and one learner starts the story, with each player in the group continuing the story depending on what they have on their cards.
Variation 2: students can take their three cards home and for homework they can write out their story, record it and bring in the recording, or create a mime of the story to show their group/classmates.

23. Sounds Like . . .
This activity is a sorting activity played in groups of 5 or 6. Each group has a topic pack of cards.
Spread out all the cards, and each player chooses a sound/letter and then tries to collect all the topic cards with that beginning sound/letter. Once all the cards have been taken by members of the team, each member of the team says the words on the card they have collected. The rest of the team then checks to see if the cards collected are right and fit the sound/letter correctly.

24. Syllables
This activity is a sorting activity played in groups of 4. Each group has a topic pack of cards.
Spread out all the cards, and each player chooses a number of syllables—one, two, three or four, and then tries to collect all the topic cards with words of that number of syllables. Once all the cards have been taken by members of the team, each member of the team says the words on the cards they have collected, and the rest of the team checks to see if the cards collected are correct for the number of syllables.

25. Spelling Pairs

Pairwork

Each pair has a number of cards linked to a topic or a mixture of topics the class has covered so far in the year. Each partner takes a card (without letting their partner see what is on the card) and asks their partner to spell the word on the card. If they do so correctly, the 'speller' partner gets the card.

26. I Like/Don't Like . . .

Pairwork or group work. Topic cards, or a mixture of topic cards, are shared between the pair or group.

Each person takes a turn to turn one of their cards over and says either 'I like…' or 'I don't like' depending on their choice, Eg. *I like chocolate. I don't like chocolate; I like reading. I don't like reading.*

27. Opposites

Pairwork

Each partner must choose a card from the sets of verbs or prepositions and put it on the desk. The other partner has to find the opposite card and put it next to the first card. After the game is played the teacher asks all the pairs to let her/him know how many pairs of cards they managed to find and the pairs with the most pairs of cards win the activity.

How about your suggestions? Contact us!

The different ways to use the Mini Flashcards are endless, as you can easily adapt and extend the games and activities in this book, or simply invent your own. Or maybe your students will suggest some! If you want to share these new ideas, we'd love to hear from you.

Write to **english@northstarelt.co.uk** and we can put your ideas on the website to share with other teachers. Or you can go to the website to see what others have done with these fabulous resources. Visit **www.northstarelt.co.uk/miniflashcards**.

Have fun!

Mini Flashcards Language Games

The Mini Flashcards featured in this book are:

Mini Flashcards Language Games — **Adjectives**
978-1-907584-07-7

Mini Flashcards Language Games — **All About Me**
978-1-907584-08-4

Mini Flashcards Language Games — **At Home**
978-1-907584-09-1

Mini Flashcards Language Games — **At School**
978-1-907584-10-7

Mini Flashcards Language Games — **Body & Health**
978-1-907584-11-4

Mini Flashcards Language Games — **Clothes**
978-1-907584-12-1

Mini Flashcards Language Games — **Feelings**
978-1-907584-13-8

Mini Flashcards Language Games — **Food & Drink**
978-1-907584-14-5

Mini Flashcards Language Games — **Happy Holidays**
978-1-907584-15-2

Mini Flashcards Language Games — **Leisure**
978-1-907584-16-9

Mini Flashcards Language Games — **People & Jobs**
978-1-907584-17-6

Mini Flashcards Language Games — **Prepositions & Directions**
978-1-907584-18-3

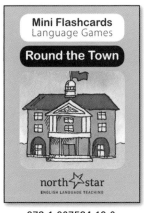

Mini Flashcards Language Games — **Round the Town**
978-1-907584-19-0

Mini Flashcards Language Games — **Travel**
978-1-907584-20-6

Mini Flashcards Language Games — **Verbs**
978-1-907584-21-3

Mini Flashcards Language Games — **Weather & Calendar**
978-1-907584-22-0

For free sample materials and more information, contact **english@northstarelt.co.uk** or visit **www.northstarelt.co.uk/miniflashcards**

Word List: Adjectives

1.	round / square	21.	comfortable / uncomfortable
2.	rectangular / triangular	22.	wet / dry
3.	straight / curved	23.	clean / dirty
4.	large / medium / small	24.	tidy / untidy
5.	long / short	25.	full / empty
6.	thick / thin	26.	deep / shallow
7.	narrow / wide	27.	high / low
8.	heavy / light	28.	busy / quiet
9.	hard / soft	29.	shut / open
10.	rough / smooth	30.	vacant / engaged
11.	light / dark	31.	present / absent
12.	glass / plastic	32.	delicious / horrible
13.	wooden / metal	33.	fun / boring
14.	paper	34.	wonderful / terrible
15.	fast / slow	35.	dangerous / safe
16.	loud / quiet	36.	same / different
17.	hot / cold	37.	easy / difficult
18.	expensive / cheap	38.	right / wrong
19.	new / old	39.	first / last
20.	beautiful / ugly	40.	fair / unfair

Language Games

In addition to the ideas in the section *Activities & Games for using the Mini Flashcards and Picture Pages* you can try these extra ideas for *Adjectives*:

1 True or False

Pairwork or groups of 3-4

Players choose a card and make a sentence about one of the items shown in that picture, using one of the adjectives describing it. Eg. *The tortoise is slow*. They can be *true* or *false* statements, which the other player has to answer 'true' or 'false'. Then they can use the adjective to describe something else not on the card: Eg. *Snails are slow*.

Then they can turn the adjectives into comparatives or superlatives to make more sentences. Eg. *France is bigger than Portugal. Russia is bigger than France and Portugal. Russia is the biggest.*

2 Guessing Games

Pairwork or groups of 3-4

Players describe a picture on a chosen card (or on the picture handout) without mentioning the adjectives. Player B has to name the two adjectives (groups: the first player to name the two adjectives wins). Eg. *One jumper costs £5, the other costs £500* (cheap/expensive).

Variation 1: Describe any object. Eg. *It's green, made of plastic, it has pens in it* (pencil case).

Variation 2: You think of an object. The other players have 20 yes/no questions to find out what it is. Eg. *Is it made of plastic? Is it made of paper? Is it round? Is it big?*

Players can answer *yes* or *no*, but they can also say things like *sometimes*, *it depends*, etc.

© 2010 North Star ELT   **Mini Flashcards Language Games: Teacher's Book** (ISBN 978-1-907584-03-9)   www.northstarelt.co.uk

③ I Went to the Shops . . .

Groups of 3-4 (see Activities & Games)
When the learners are listing the items they bought, they should use an adjective (pick a card or picture from the handout) to describe it in more detail such as the following:
Learner 1: *I went to the shops and I bought an expensive watch.*
Learner 2: *I went to the shops and I bought an expensive watch and a beautiful dress.*
Learner 3: *I went to the shops and I bought an expensive watch, a beautiful dress and an old car . . .*

④ What can you see?

Pairwork or groups of 3-4
A player picks a card (or chooses a picture from the handout) and has to describe thing(s) in the classroom — or whole school! — which work with the two adjectives. Eg. *The windows are dirty. The door is shut. My teacher is wonderful!* They could do the same activity about things at home.

⑤ Magazine pictures

Groups of 3-4
Ask the class to bring in large pictures of things or places which are stuck on the walls around the classroom. The learners go round making a list of adjectives for each one, and sticking them on the wall next to the magazine pictures. Alternatively, you can give them each a set of photocopied cut-outs of all the adjectives, and they have to stick them on the wall next to appropriate magazine pictures.

Word List: All About Me

1. name
2. address
3. (tele)phone number
4. birthday
5. star sign
6. nationality
7. occupation
8. sex
9. physical appearance
10. family
11. pets
12. well/not well
13. friendly
14. loner
15. calm
16. nervous
17. serious
18. silly
19. polite
20. rude
21. hard-working
22. lazy
23. athletic
24. cowardly
25. brave
26. messy
27. noisy
28. bad-tempered
29. proud
30. impatient
31. naughty
32. sympathetic
33. affectionate
34. charming
35. generous
36. artistic
37. imaginative
38. honest
39. romantic
40. optimistic/ pessimistic

Language Games

Cards / pictures 1-12 are the kinds items of personal information often requested on forms or questionnaires to fill in. Cards/pictures 13-40 are personality traits.

In addition to the ideas in the section *Activities & Games for using the Mini Flashcards and Picture Pages* you can try these extra ideas for *All About Me*:

① My friends

Individual and group work
The learner makes a list of 3 of their friends. They find the cards from *All About Me* that describe the qualities of each of these friends and write these down. When this is finished, the learners can give their friends these lists of their qualities, or they have to guess who is who.

② Guessing Games

Pairwork or groups of 3-4
Players choose a card or picture and describe things people do to be the word they have. The other(s) have to guess.
Eg. *He writes poems for his girlfriend and always buys her flowers* (romantic).
She never tidies her room. Her hands are always dirty (messy).

© 2010 North Star ELT **Mini Flashcards Language Games** (ISBN 978-1-907584-03-9) www.northstarelt.co.uk

③ Chain game

Groups of 3-4 (this is a variation on *I Went to the Shops . . .*)
Instead of objects you buy, the game is about describing people. Players pick cards and let those words be the prompts:
Learner 1: *I know a person who is athletic.*
Learner 2: *I know a person who is athletic and honest.*
Learner 3: *I know a person who is athletic, honest, and calm. . . etc.*

④ TV personalities

Groups of 4-6
Each group thinks of a famous person from TV. Each player lists (from the word list) 3 qualities they think their personality has. Then they discuss with the rest of the group what qualities they all thought of and agree on a final 3 for the whole group. Give another group the 3 qualities, and that group has to guess which TV personality was chosen. They could stick the list of qualities on the wall with a photo of the TV personality.

⑤ Matching the job

Groups of 3-4
With the *People & Jobs* cards, the group chooses 3 jobs from the cards and then decides what qualities are needed to do this job. Eg. Policeman: *brave, athletic, friendly . . . etc.*

⑥ Castaways

Pairwork
Learners use the cards or pictures to prompt the qualities of 1 perfect person they would like to be with, if they were a castaway on a desert island.

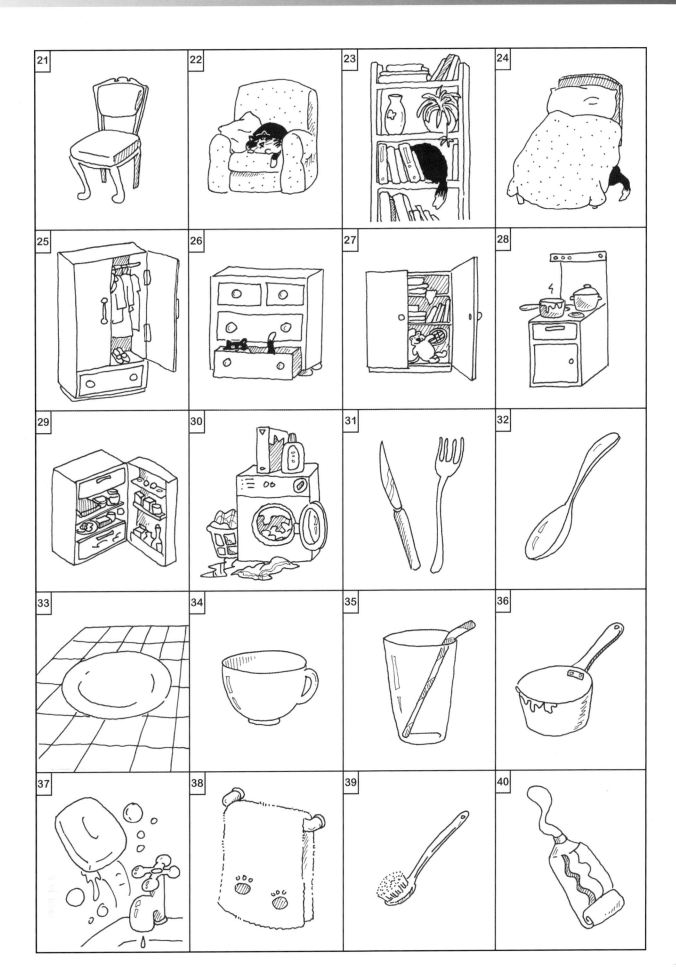

© 2010 North Star ELT   **Mini Flashcards Language Games: Teacher's Book** (ISBN 978-1-907584-03-9)   www.northstarelt.co.uk

Word List: At Home

1.	door	21.	chair
2.	window	22.	armchair
3.	stairs	23.	shelves
4.	garage	24.	bed
5.	garden	25.	wardrobe
6.	hall	26.	chest of drawers
7.	living room	27.	cupboard
8.	dining room	28.	cooker
9.	kitchen	29.	fridge
10.	bedroom	30.	washing machine
11.	bathroom	31.	knife (and) fork
12.	radiator	32.	spoon
13.	carpet	33.	plate
14.	curtains	34.	cup
15.	mirror	35.	glass
16.	picture	36.	(sauce)pan
17.	lamp	37.	soap
18.	(tele)phone	38.	towel
19.	alarm clock	39.	toothbrush
20.	table	40.	toothpaste

Language Games

In addition to the ideas in the section *Activities & Games for using the Mini Flashcards and Picture Pages* you can try these extra ideas for *At Home*:

❶ Chain game

Groups of 3-4 (this is a variation on *I Went to the Shops . . .*)
Instead of objects you buy to eat, the game is about things to buy for the house. Players pick cards and let those words be the prompts:
Learner 1: *I went to the shops and bought a mirror.*
Learner 2: *I went to the shops and bought a mirror and a lamp.*
Learner 3: *I went to the shops and bought a mirror, a lamp and a picture.*

❷ Bedroom Survey

Groups of 6 or whole class
Learners think of questions to ask about each other's bedrooms, based on the picture prompts. Eg. *Have you got a mirror in your bedroom? Do you share your bedroom with a brother/sister?* At the end of the survey learners should collate the answers and feed back to the group or class. Eg. *3 people in our group share their bedroom with a sister or brother. Everyone in our group has got a mirror in their bedroom.*

© 2010 North Star ELT   **Mini Flashcards Language Games: Teacher's Book** (ISBN 978-1-907584-03-9)   www.northstarelt.co.uk

③ My home

Pairwork

Learners choose cards or pictures to prompt them to talk or write about their home, or just their bedroom.

Variation: Learners choose cards to prompt them to talk or write about their perfect home. Eg. *My perfect home has got 8 bedrooms and a giant mirror in the hall. The garden is very big and has got a swimming pool. There is red carpet on the stairs, etc.* They can draw a plan or picture of the house and give it labels.

④ Chores

Groups of 3-4

Learners choose cards or pictures to prompt them to talk or write about the chores or jobs they have to do around the house, or routines at home.

⑤ What can you see?

Pairwork or groups of 3-4

A player picks a card (or chooses a picture from the handout) and has to talk about what they see in the room - or whole house! Eg. *There is a fridge in the kitchen. There is a bed and a wardrobe in the bedroom. I see a table and some chairs in the dining room.*

Word List: At School

1. teacher	21. (black)board
2. pupil	22. CD player
3. classroom	23. English
4. laboratory (lab)	24. French
5. gym	25. German
6. dining hall	26. Spanish
7. playground	27. maths
8. break	28. biology
9. (text)book	29. chemistry
10. dictionary	30. physics
11. exercise book	31. history
12. paper	32. geography
13. pen	33. design & technology (DT)
14. pencil	34. information technology (IT)
15. pencil sharpener	35. music
16. rubber	36. art
17. ruler	37. physical education (PE)
18. calculator	38. timetable
19. pencil case	39. examination (exam)
20. school bag	40. homework

Language Games

In addition to the ideas in the section *Activities & Games for using the Mini Flashcards and Picture Pages* you can try these extra ideas for *At School*:

1 Chain game

Groups of 3-4 (this is a variation on *I Went to the Shops . . .*)
Instead of objects you buy to eat, the game is about things in your school bag. Players pick cards and let those words be the prompts:
Learner 1: *In my school bag I've got a pencil.*
Learner 2: *In my school bag I've got a pencil and a ruler.*
Learner 3: *In my school bag I've got a pencil, a ruler and a calculator.*

2 Surveys

Groupwork or whole class
• Surveys of what people have on their desks, in pencil cases, in school bags.
• Survey to find the most/least attractive school bag/pencil cases.
• Survey of most/least favourite lessons.
• Survey of what time and where people do their homework.

3 Timetables

Pairwork or groupwork
Learners talk about their usual school timetable or layout, and then create their ideal school timetable or layout. Pairs or groups mix to compare ideas.

© 2010 North Star ELT **Mini Flashcards Language Games: Teacher's Book** (ISBN 978-1-907584-03-9) www.northstarelt.co.uk

4 School subjects

Pairwork
Learners pick cards/pictures from 23–37 and talk about what they like/dislike about these subjects, and why.

5 Directions

Pairwork
Using the *Prepositions & Directions* pictures or cards, learners describe how to get from one room to another at school, or how to get home from school. Partners have to check to see if their partner's answer is correct. Players could make a map of the school or route home before they play the game.

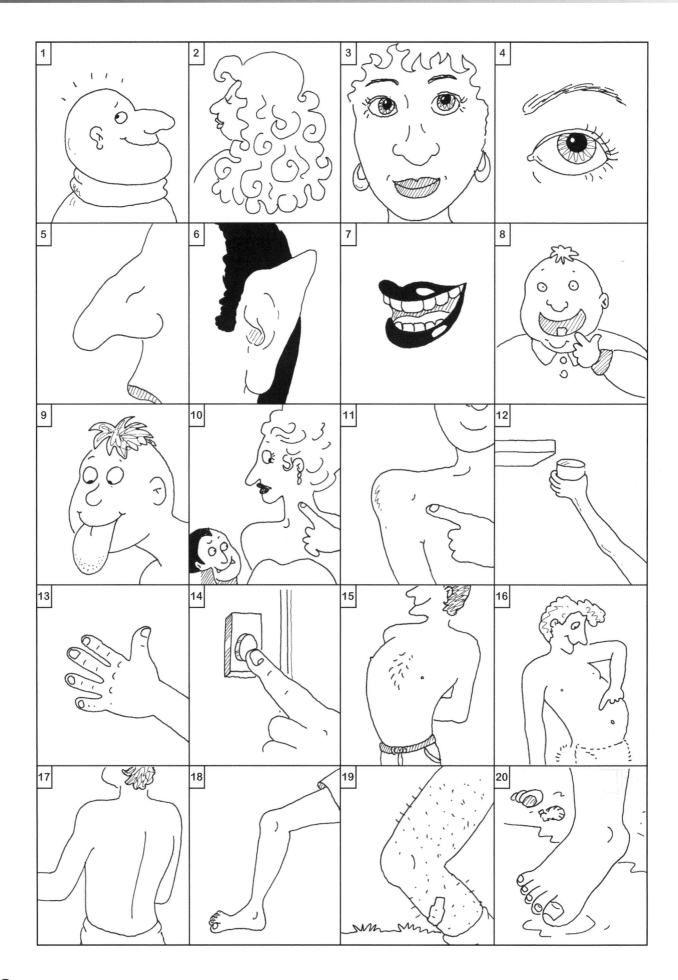

© 2010 North Star ELT   **Mini Flashcards Language Games: Teacher's Book** (ISBN 978-1-907584-03-9)   www.northstarelt.co.uk

Word List: Body & Health

1. head	21. toe
2. hair	22. I'm hungry
3. face	23. I'm thirsty
4. eye	24. I feel dizzy
5. nose	25. I've got a nosebleed
6. ear	26. I've got a cold
7. mouth	27. I've got a temperature
8. tooth	28. I've got indigestion
9. tongue	29. I'm being sick
10. neck	30. I feel sea sick
11. shoulder	31. I've got a toothache
12. arm	32. I've got a sunburn
13. hand	33. I've got spots
14. finger	34. I've got a backache
15. chest	35. I've broken my leg
16. stomach	36. I've sprained my ankle
17. back	37. I've bumped my head
18. leg	38. I've cut myself
19. knee	39. I've burnt myself
20. foot	40. I've been stung

Language Games

In addition to the ideas in the section *Activities & Games for using the Mini Flashcards and Picture Pages* you can try these extra ideas for *Body & Health*:

❶ Matching Pairs 1

Pairwork or groups of 3-4

Use the *Body & Health* cards with the *Clothes* cards. All the cards are put on the desk, spread out. Each player has to select some 'body' cards to match with cards showing health problems or *Clothes* cards and explain why they have matched these cards, or they can tell a story.

Eg. *stomach – sick, sea sick, indigestion*

back – T-shirt, shirt, coat, etc

foot – boot, shoe, sock, etc

My new boots are too big and yesterday I tripped and sprained my ankle.

The partner or rest of the group should decide if they accept the match. If they do, the player or group keeps the cards. If not, then the cards are put back on the table.

❷ Matching Pairs 2

Pairwork or group work

Using the *Body & Health* cards with *Verbs* cards or *Leisure* cards, agree in advance a list of activities and one part of body needed to carry them out. Players then list these activities on slips of paper and use them to play 'matching pairs' with the cards.

Eg. *football – foot, typing – finger, tennis – arm*

© 2010 North Star ELT **Mini Flashcards Language Games: Teacher's Book** (ISBN 978-1-907584-03-9) www.northstarelt.co.uk

3 At the Doctor's

Pairwork

Role-play using cards 24-40. Learners take turns to be doctor and patient. Keep the cards in a pile, face up. The learners greet each other (*Good Morning*, etc. Doctor asks *What seems to be trouble?* Or *How are you today?* Student B picks up the first card and uses the prompt to act out his/her problem and say what's wrong. *I'm not feeling well, Doctor. I feel dizzy.* The doctor asks questions to find out more, then recommends a remedy. Eg. *Take these tablets and go and lie down.*

4 Blog/Diary

Working alone or pairwork

Using cards 24-40, ask students to pick a card and write a blog or diary entry for someone with one or more of the health problems.
Eg. *I am walking in the park. I feel a pain on my leg. I look at my leg. I've been stung by a bee.*

5 Surveys

Whole class

Students carry one of the cards and then walk round the class, ask their classmates questions, keeping notes of the answers.
Eg. *Did you ever have a toothache? Did you ever feel sea sick?*
After the survey, students should be ready to present the information they've collected.

© 2010 North Star ELT   **Mini Flashcards Language Games: Teacher's Book** (ISBN 978-1-907584-03-9)   www.northstarelt.co.uk

Word List: Clothes

1.	clothes	21.	tights
2.	coat	22.	socks
3.	raincoat	23.	pyjamas / nightdress
4.	anorak	24.	tracksuit
5.	jacket	25.	leotard
6.	suit	26.	swimming costume
7.	jumper	27.	boots
8.	cardigan	28.	shoes
9.	top	29.	sandals
10.	dress	30.	trainers
11.	skirt	31.	tie
12.	trousers	32.	belt
13.	jeans	33.	(hand)bag
14.	blouse	34.	scarf
15.	shirt	35.	hat
16.	T-shirt	36.	(pair of) glasses
17.	shorts	37.	watch
18.	knickers	38.	purse / wallet
19.	underpants	39.	size (of clothes)
20.	bra	40.	size (of shoes)

Language Games

In addition to the ideas in the section *Activities & Games for using the Mini Flashcards and Picture Pages* you can try these extra ideas for *Clothes*:

① Quick Flash

Class/group work or pairs

Teacher or group leader quickly flashes a picture of clothing to the group and they have to try and describe what it is by name and description. Eg. *It's a shirt.* The players should then continue with colour and pattern: *It's a red striped shirt.* The player with the longest and most fitting description (or who can say the most) keeps the card. The winner is the person with the most cards at the end of the game.

② Chain Game Variation

Groups of 3-4

A learner starts the chain sentence as in the game 'I went to market' but this time they link it to going on holiday, going to a party, or going to school.
Eg.
Learner 1: *I went on holiday and I took... a pair of shorts.*
Learner 2: *I went on holiday and I took a pair of shorts and a T-shirt.*
Learner 3: *I went on holiday and I took a pair of shorts, a T-shirt and swimming costume.*

Learner 1: *I went to a party and I wore a suit.*
Learner 2: *I went to a party and I wore a suit and a tie.*
Learner 3: *I went to a party and I wore a suit, a tie and a belt.*

© 2010 North Star ELT Mini Flashcards Language Games: Teacher's Book (ISBN 978-1-907584-03-9) www.northstarelt.co.uk

③ How much is it?

Pairwork

Using the handout of pictures or any selection of cards, learners decide on prices for things. They act out a role play where one student is a customer and the other is the shop assistant.

Student A: *Have you got any watches?*
Student B: *Yes. We have these.*
Student A: *How much is this one?*
Student B: *This one's £75.*
Student A: *I'm sorry. That's too expensive. Do you have a cheaper one? etc.*

④ What is it?

Pairwork or groups of 3-4

Put a pack of cards (or a selection) in a pile face up, but only one student (or the leader if it is a group) can see them. He/she picks up the top card and describes what the clothing item is for. The other learners have to guess. Learners keep the cards if they guess correctly. You can do this with the black and white handouts, where the 'caller' describes what a clothing item is for, and the others guess the object and/or say the number. Eg. *You wear them when you go to bed* – answer: *pyjamas.*

⑤ At the Mall

Pairwork

Role-play using the cards. Learners take it in turns to be clerk and customer. Keep the cards in a pile, face up. The learners greet each other *Good morning*, etc. Clerk asks *How can I help you?* OR *What are you looking for today?* The customer picks up the first card and uses the prompt to ask for an item. *I am looking for a dress.* The clerk asks questions to find out more information about the item. *What colour dress are you looking for?*, *Do you want a long dress or a short dress?* The customer answers. *I am looking for a long, black dress.* Then the clerk recommends an item. Eg. *Here is a beautiful long, black dress. It only costs £45.*

© 2010 North Star ELT **Mini Flashcards Language Games: Teacher's Book** (ISBN 978-1-907584-03-9) www.northstarelt.co.uk

Word List: Feelings

1.	flowers	21.	happy
2.	postcard	22.	angry
3.	Valentine's card	23.	confused
4.	letter	24.	guilty
5.	phone call	25.	embarrassed
6.	knock at the door	26.	sad
7.	dream	27.	suspicious
8.	(make) a wish	28.	shy
9.	small present	29.	shocked
10.	present	30.	lonely
11.	large present	31.	jealous
12.	kiss	32.	fed up
13.	hug	33.	disappointed
14.	argument	34.	scared
15.	smile	35.	disgusted
16.	photo(graph)	36.	rejected
17.	(to go on) a date	37.	excited
18.	in love	38.	worried
19.	broken-hearted	39.	annoyed
20.	passionate	40.	clumsy

Language Games

In addition to the ideas in the section *Activities & Games for using the Mini Flashcards and Picture Pages* you can try these extra ideas for *Feelings*:

1 Prompting Feelings

Pairwork or groups of 3-4
Spread out some of the *Feelings* cards on one part of a table. In pairs, players choose a card and make a sentence.

Eg. *I feel excited when I go on holiday.*
I feel happy when I get a birthday card from a friend.
I feel shy when I go to a party.
I feel annoyed when I have to go to bed.

2 True stories

Pairwork
Using cards (or photocopied pictures) 18-40, ask the students to talk in the past tense about true moments (separate or connected) when they had some of these feelings. Students can report back to the class, or write about their partner's experiences as a story.

Eg. *Maria was **fed up** last week because she was **worried** that her boyfriend was going out with someone else. She was **jealous** and **angry**.*

As an alternative or extension exercise, learners could make up a story using as many of the prompts as possible.

© 2010 North Star ELT   **Mini Flashcards Language Games: Teacher's Book** (ISBN 978-1-907584-03-9)   www.northstarelt.co.uk

❸ Who's it from?

Pairwork or groups of 3-4

Pairs or groups have cards 1-11 only scattered in front of them, and some of cards 18-40 in a pile separately. One person closes their eyes and cards 1-11 are moved around, and then that person chooses a card from them. The pair/group then have to make up a story starting with that object, and using the other cards as prompts for feelings.

❹ Films & Books

Pairwork or groups of 3-4

Ask the groups to list some of their favourite films and/or books. Using cards (or photocopied pictures) 18-40, they have to talk about the feelings of some of the main characters at various points in the stories, and why they feel the way they do.

❺ A Memorable Day

Working alone or pairwork

Ask the students to make up a story about the best or worst day they had recently. They should tell what happened and how they felt about it.

Eg. *My best friend called me last week. She lives very far away. We talked for an hour. I was so happy. That was a great day!*

Word List: Food & Drink

1.	bread	21.	orange
2.	butter	22.	apple
3.	jam	23.	lemon
4.	sandwich	24.	dessert
5.	cheese	25.	cake
6.	ham	26.	ice-cream
7.	sausage	27.	sweet
8.	egg	28.	milk
9.	salt (and) pepper	29.	tea
10.	meat	30.	coffee
11.	soup	31.	sugar
12.	chicken	32.	mineral water
13.	fish	33.	(fruit) juice
14.	vegetable	34.	lemonade
15.	peas	35.	hot chocolate
16.	potato	36.	soft / fizzy drink
17.	salad	37.	chocolate
18.	chips	38.	breakfast
19.	fruit	39.	lunch
20.	strawberry	40.	dinner

Language Games

In addition to the ideas in the section *Activities & Games for using the Mini Flashcards and Picture Pages* you can try these extra ideas for *Food & Drink*:

1 I Went to Market

Groups of 3-4

Spread some appropriate cards out on the table. One learner starts a sentence and the next learner repeats the sentence from memory and adds an item. If a player can't remember a word, the others can help by prompting him/her with their mini flashcard.
Eg.
Learner 1: *I went to market and bought a cake.*
Learner 2: *I went to market and bought a cake and some milk.*
Learner 3: *I went to market and bought a cake, some milk and an apple.*

2 Healthy Meals

Groups of 5

Each group should have five or six randomly chosen cards from the topic. They then use the cards, whatever they are, to decide if they show healthy or unhealthy food. In their group they should decide which foods in their cards are healthier than others and why.

© 2010 North Star ELT **Mini Flashcards Language Games: Teacher's Book** (ISBN 978-1-907584-03-9) www.northstarelt.co.uk

❸ Table Talk

Pairwork

Role play. Spread out a random selection of six of the topic cards in the middle of the table with the pictures face up. The two learners should then use them to prompt a dialogue.

Eg.　**Student A:** *Would you like another sandwich?*
　　　Student B: *No, thank you. But could I have another piece of cake?*
　　　Student A: *Yes, of course. Here you are.*
　　　Student B: *Thank you. Delicious!*

The teacher should go around listening to the pairs, and choose some pairs to do their conversation for the whole class. They should hold up their pictures as they speak about the food so the class can see what is on the picture.

❹ Menu Planning

Groups of 4-5

The group has at least 20 cards and spreads them out on a desk so that they can all see them. They then have to create five balanced meals from this selection, and create a written and illustrated menu to go with them. On the board or wall, the teacher makes a display of all the menus.

❺ Favourite Food Survey

Groups of 3

Each member of the group should have some cards which show food related to *breakfast*, *lunch* or *dinner*. They should go round the class and ask at least five other people if they have any of these foods for their breakfast, lunch or dinner. After the survey they must be ready to tell their findings to the group or whole class.

Word List: Happy Holidays

1.	camp(ing) site	21.	menu
2.	tent	22.	sunglasses
3.	youth hostel	23.	swimming shorts / swimsuit
4.	rucksack	24.	towel
5.	hotel	25.	suncream
6.	reception	26.	(swimming) pool
7.	single room	27.	beach
8.	double room	28.	café
9.	bath(room)	29.	bill
10.	shower	30.	money
11.	toilet	31.	tourist office
12.	balcony	32.	map
13.	view	33.	street map
14.	passport	34.	excursion
15.	key	35.	camera
16.	suitcase	36.	video camera
17.	lift	37.	souvenir
18.	breakfast	38.	postcard
19.	bar	39.	stamp
20.	restaurant	40.	postbox

Language Games

In addition to the ideas in the section *Activities & Games for using the Mini Flashcards and Picture Pages* you can try these extra ideas for *Happy Holidays*:

❶ Two's Company

Pairwork

Role play. One student is the hotel receptionist, another is the guest. Ten appropriate cards are dealt to the guest as prompts to the conversation. The guest then has to ask the hotel receptionist to help them.

Eg. *Camera* (lost / broken my camera / where can I buy…)

Excursion (how long? how much? where? what to see? clothing?)

Shower (not working / too hot / there isn't a shower / there's a giant spider)

An alternative scenario could be Travel Agent & Customer.

❷ Memories

Pairwork

Students look through the cards to find ones which prompt memories of their favourite or worst holiday. Then they put the cards in the correct order for the other learner to tell the memories back to their partner. Have learners write them up for homework or share stories with the rest of the class.

© 2010 North Star ELT **Mini Flashcards Language Games: Teacher's Book** (ISBN 978-1-907584-03-9) www.northstarelt.co.uk

③ Holiday Disaster

Pairwork

Students pretend they (or a friend) have been on a terrible holiday where everything went wrong. They have to choose (or the teacher gives them) six cards at random, and the students use the prompts to tell their stories.

④ Guessing Games

Pairwork or groups of 3-4

Players describe the object on a chosen card (or on a picture handout). The other players have to name the object. The player who names the object correctly keeps the card. The player with the most cards at the end of the game is the winner. Eg. *You eat this in the morning. It is the most important meal of the day.* Answer: *breakfast*

Variation 1: You think of an object. The other players ask 20 *yes / no* questions to find out what it is. Eg. *Is it food? Do you eat it in the morning?*
Players can answer *yes* or *no*, but they can also say things like *sometimes*, *it depends*, etc.

⑤ Blog/Diary

Working alone or pairwork

Ask the students to make up a blog or diary entry about a holiday that have taken recently. They can talk about where they went, where they stayed and if they enjoyed the holiday. Ask them to give as many details as they can.

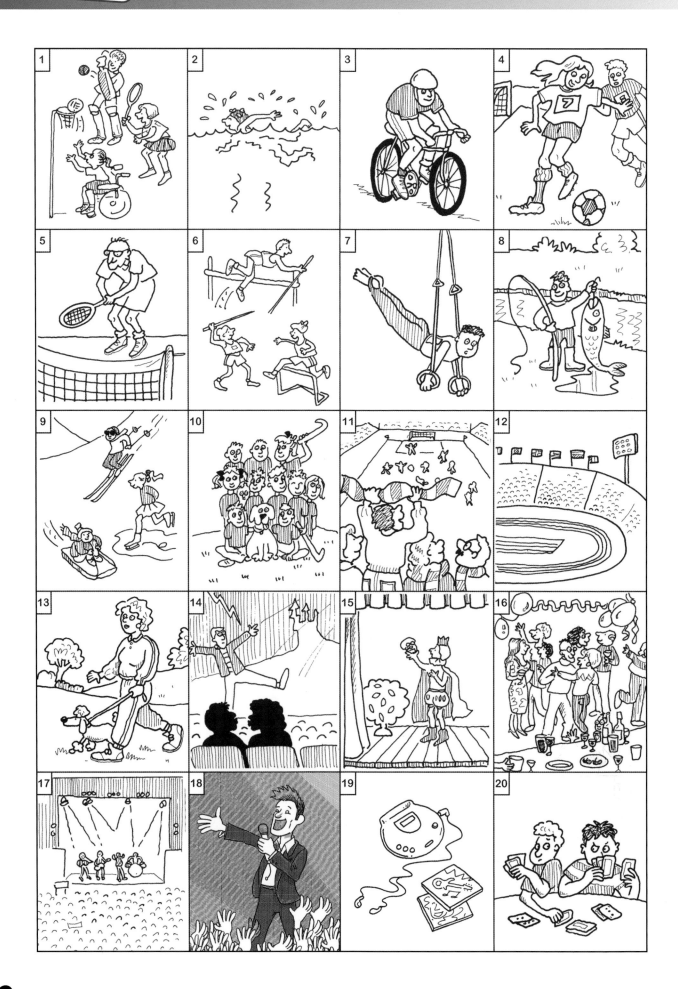

Word List: Leisure

1.	sport	21.	chess
2.	swimming	22.	toy
3.	cycling	23.	photography
4.	football	24.	DIY (do-it-yourself)
5.	tennis	25.	gardening
6.	athletics	26.	radio
7.	gymnastics	27.	television (TV)
8.	fishing	28.	DVD
9.	winter sports	29.	computer
10.	team	30.	relaxation
11.	match	31.	(news)paper
12.	stadium	32.	magazine
13.	a walk	33.	fashion
14.	cinema	34.	dog
15.	theatre	35.	cat
16.	party	36.	horse
17.	concert	37.	rabbit
18.	pop star	38.	bird
19.	CD	39.	fish
20.	cards	40.	mouse

Language Games

In addition to the ideas in the section *Activities & Games for using the Mini Flashcards and Picture Pages* you can try these extra ideas for *Leisure*:

❶ At the Sports Centre

Groups of 4-5

A learner starts the chain sentence as in the game 'I went to market' but this time they link it to leisure activities.

Eg. **Learner 1:** *At the leisure centre I play football.*
Learner 2: *At the leisure centre I play football and go swimming.*
Learner 3: *At the leisure centre I play football, (and then I) go swimming, (and then I) play tennnis.*

❷ Matching Pairs: Hobbies

Pairwork or Group work

Choose some cards from a selection of about 20, whilst the partner (or group) writes sentences about these hobbies/leisure activities on pieces of paper. Another pair or group have to match these up to the pictures.

Eg. *It's very peaceful. You have time to think. = fishing*
You fall down a lot and get very cold. = skiing

© 2010 North Star ELT **Mini Flashcards Language Games: Teacher's Book** (ISBN 978-1-907584-03-9) www.northstarelt.co.uk

❸ Surveys

Whole class

Students carry one of the cards and move around asking their classmates questions, keeping a note on a grid or chart (Eg. who owns a pet, favourite sports/leisure activities, favourite music, favourite TV programmes). After the survey, students should be ready to present the information they collected, Eg. *Eight people in the class have cats and 3 people have dogs. Favourite sports are football, swimming and skateboarding.*
More people prefer pop music to classical music.

❹ How Often?

Pairwork

With a partner, the learners go through a selection of these cards, saying whether they do these things *often*, *sometimes*, *occasionally* or *never*. Put the cards into *often*, *sometimes*, *occasionally* or *never* piles on the desk and see how many are in each pile. Learners compare their use of leisure time.

❺ My Favourite

Pairwork

Learners choose cards or pictures to prompt them to talk or write about their favourite leisure activities.
They should talk about when they like to do these activities, where they do these activities, and why they like these activities.
Eg. *There is a river near my house. I like to go fishing there on the weekends. I like to go fishing because it is very quiet and peaceful.*

Word List: People & Jobs

1.	woman	21.	vet
2.	man	22.	baker
3.	friend	23.	receptionist
4.	girlfriend / boyfriend	24.	shop assistant
5.	neighbour	25.	musician
6.	pensioner	26.	butcher
7.	househusband / housewife	27.	policeman / policewoman
8.	pupil	28.	chemist
9.	student	29.	bank clerk
10.	unemployed	30.	farmer
11.	customer	31.	nurse
12.	tourist	32.	artist
13.	computer programmer	33.	waiter / waitress
14.	postman / postwoman	34.	customs officer
15.	engineer	35.	taxi driver
16.	doctor	36.	chef
17.	dentist	37.	teacher
18.	flight attendant	38.	mechanic
19.	fireman / firewoman	39.	hairdresser
20.	office worker	40.	builder

Language Games

In addition to the ideas in the section *Activities & Games for using the Mini Flashcards and Picture Pages* you can try these extra ideas for *People & Jobs*:

1 What am I?

2 groups, with 2-4 players in a group

One player takes a card (not showing it to anyone) and mimes the job on the card. The other player(s) ask up to 10 questions to find out what the job is. S/he can only answer *yes* or *no*. If the other player(s) guess the job correctly, they win a point and take the next turn. Points are lost for wrong guesses. If, after 10 questions, the guessing player(s) cannot guess the job correctly, the first player/team wins the point, and s/he(or another member of the team) takes another card and does another mime.

2 Detectives

Group work

Stick 15 cards on the board (or use enlarged cut-out photocopies of 15 pictures from the selection in this unit). Tell the students you are a witness to a robbery. You describe one of the characters on the cards to the class (who are the detectives) and the first one to guess who it is correctly is the winner. This game can then be played in groups with players taking it in turns to be the games person.

Variation: You can put the pictures on the walls around the classroom and, first, let the students walk around to see what the people in the pictures look like. Then, when you describe the person, the students have to walk over and stand by/under the picture of the person who they think it is.

© 2010 North Star ELT **Mini Flashcards Language Games: Teacher's Book** (ISBN 978-1-907584-03-9) www.northstarelt.co.uk

3 What are they saying?

Pairwork or Group work

Stick 10 cards of people with jobs on the walls around the classroom (or even use enlarged cut-out photocopies of 10 pictures from the selection in this unit). Ask the learners to walk around to see what all the jobs are. Then, in pairs or groups, ask the learners to write a speech bubble for each person in a picture, and then stick them by that picture (Eg. for Chef: *Oh no! I've burnt the steaks!* or *I need some onions.* Flight Attendant: *We're going to land in twenty minutes* or *Can you put your bag under the seat in front of you?*). Learners walk around to see each other's examples. They can read them out loud to each other.

4 Job Descriptions

Pairwork or Group work

In pairs or groups, one of the learners takes a card, hiding it from the other players. They write a list of five things that the person might do in his/her job, Eg. waiter: *takes orders, brings food to the table, prepares a bill, takes money, clears the table*. The others guess who it is. One point for the person who guesses correctly. Points lost for wrong guesses. The winner is the player with the most points at the end of the game.

5 Conversations

Pairwork

Two players each take a card, then role-play a conversation that might take place between the two people. Eg.

- doctor treating a farmer who has hurt his/her back
- woman complaining to a mechanic that her car hasn't been fixed properly
- musician going to the chemist because she has a sore throat

6 Job Interview

Groups of 4

One player wants a new job, and is given a card which everyone can see. The other three players are the interviewers and can ask the interviewee about such things as:

- how much they know about the job
- why they want the job
- why they think they would be good at the job
- do they have similar experience

The applicants then have an opportunity to ask questions (Eg. about training, the organisation, the hours, the pay). The interviewers then decides if they will give the job to the interviewee.

7 Blog/Diary

Working alone or pairwork

Ask the students to pick a card and write a blog or diary entry for one of the people, describing some of their daily, weekly and monthly routines.

8 A Memorable Day

Working alone or pairwork

Ask the students to pick a card and make up a story about the best or worst day that person had in their job. They can pretend to be the person in the card and write from their point of view.

Word List: Prepositions and Directions

1.	where's . . .?	21.	behind
2.	(over) here	22.	next to
3.	(over) there	23.	between
4.	near (to)	24.	(on) either side (of)
5.	far (from)	25.	against
6.	straight on	26.	opposite
7.	left	27.	at the end (of)
8.	right	28.	at the edge (of)
9.	first left	29.	in the middle (of)
10.	second left	30.	at the back (of)
11.	third right	31.	in the corner (of)
12.	(go) over	32.	on the wall
13.	(go) under	33.	on the floor
14.	(go) through	34.	at the top (of)
15.	to, towards	35.	at the bottom (of)
16.	from	36.	upstairs / on the first floor
17.	in	37.	downstairs / on the ground floor
18.	on	38.	outside
19.	under	39.	inside
20.	in front (of)	40.	at my / X's house

Language Games

In addition to the ideas in the section *Activities & Games for using the Mini Flashcards and Picture Pages* you can try these extra ideas for *Prepositions & Directions*:

1 Show me the way

Pairwork or two team of 4
Use the *Prepositions & Directions* cards with *Round the Town* cards. One pair or team asks the other *Where's the bus station?* And the other team or partner has to find the prepositions to give them the correct directions from their school to the bus station. Each pair or team takes turns to ask the question. (If the players can use a map of the town/city, this would be a great way to make the answers and questions even more real and meaningful).

2 Memory Game

Groups of 5-6
Each group has a selection of appropriate *prepositions* cards. The teacher holds up a picture from a book or newspaper/ magazine and the learners look carefully at the picture for a minute. Then the teacher takes the picture away and asks questions about it. The teams should choose and hold up the correct preposition card for an answer.
Eg. Teacher: *Where was the bag?* Answer card *'on' the table*.

© 2010 North Star ELT   **Mini Flashcards Language Games: Teacher's Book** (ISBN 978-1-907584-03-9)   www.northstarelt.co.uk

❸ My Home

Pairwork

Learners look through selections of cards and choose *prepositions* as prompts to describe their own home (or combine with *At Home* cards). The partner listens and then tries to remember (and re-tell their partner) what they heard, using the cards as prompts. They can write it up and even draw a map or picture.

❹ Where is it?

Groups of 5-6

The teacher holds up a picture of a room or store from a book or newspaper/magazine and the learners look carefully at the picture. The teacher then asks where an object in the picture is located. Students take turns answering the questions.

Eg. Teacher: *Where is the vase of flowers?* Answer: *It is on the table next to the door.*

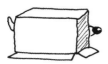   

Word List: Round the Town

1.	house	21.	bakery
2.	flat	22.	cake shop
3.	church	23.	chemist's
4.	cathedral	24.	news stand
5.	monument	25.	bookshop
6.	castle	26.	corner shop
7.	park	27.	school
8.	town hall	28.	youth club
9.	museum	29.	ice rink
10.	hospital	30.	sports centre
11.	police station	31.	cinema
12.	bank	32.	disco
13.	library	33.	restaurant
14.	post office	34.	old town
15.	office	35.	pedestrian crossing
16.	factory	36.	bus stop
17.	garage	37.	internet café
18.	shop	38.	litter bin
19.	market	39.	toilets
20.	supermarket	40.	entrance/exit

Language Games

In addition to the ideas in the section *Activities & Games for using the Mini Flashcards and Picture Pages* you can try these extra ideas for *Round the Town*:

1 My day

Groups of 4-5
A learner starts the chain sentence, as in the game 'I went to market' but this time they link it to doing things around the town.

Eg. **Learner 1:** *This morning I went to the bank.*
Learner 2: *This morning I went to the bank, and then I went to the cake shop.*
Learner 3: *This morning I went to the bank, then I went to the cake shop, and then I went to the park.*

2 Matching Pairs

Pairwork or Group work
On pieces of paper one player writes a sentence about a place for their partner or another group to match up.

Eg. *I had a game of table tennis there or I bought some cereal there or There are lots of books there.*

© 2010 North Star ELT **Mini Flashcards Language Games: Teacher's Book** (ISBN 978-1-907584-03-9) www.northstarelt.co.uk

3 New town

Groups of 3-4

Learners create their own town map using the pictures as prompts. Alternatively, they can copy their own town or area. They can use the *Prepositions & Directions* cards to to ask each other how to go from place to place.

4 Matching Pairs

Pairwork or Group work

Choose some cards from a selection of about 20. One pair (or group) writes sentences about these places on pieces of paper. Another pair or group have to match these up to the pictures.
Eg. *This place has swings and slides. = park*
    You go there to post letters and parcels. = post office

5 Role Play

Pairwork

Learners choose a card for a place and then decide on two characters who could meet there. Then they write a dialogue and role-play. The teacher can ask the class beforehand for suggested themes of the dialogues, Eg. *an argument a romantic meeting, an accident, a complaint.*

© 2010 North Star ELT **Mini Flashcards Language Games: Teacher's Book** (ISBN 978-1-907584-03-9) www.northstarelt.co.uk

Word List: Travel

1.	bike	21.	timetable
2.	motorbike	22.	luggage
3.	car	23.	lost property
4.	taxi	24.	waiting room
5.	bus	25.	toll
6.	coach	26.	petrol station
7.	lorry	27.	to fill the car with petrol
8.	train	28.	petrol
9.	underground	29.	oil
10.	ferry	30.	tyre
11.	(air)plane	31.	tram
12.	station	32.	breakdown
13.	port	33.	traffic jam
14.	airport	34.	town centre
15.	motorway	35.	street
16.	car park	36.	traffic lights
17.	traveller	37.	north
18.	on foot	38.	south
19.	ticket	39.	east
20.	ticket office	40.	west

Language Games

In addition to the ideas in the section *Activities & Games for using the Mini Flashcards and Picture Pages* you can try these extra ideas for *Travel*:

1 Destinations 1

Pairwork or group work

Learners write various destinations on pieces of paper (Eg. *the nearest post office, the nearest large town, London, Sydney, Tokyo*) and partners or other groups suggest which transport can be used to get there. Eg. *You can get there on foot or you could take a bus.*

2 Destinations 2

Pairwork or group work

Do the activity in the same way as in *Destinations 1*, but learners (without looking) take turns to take a card (from types of transport or travel) and a piece of paper (from the written destinations). Learners get a point if they make a plausible match (Eg. *Tokyo – bicycle* may not get a point unless your learners are in Japan).

© 2010 North Star ELT **Mini Flashcards Language Games: Teacher's Book** (ISBN 978-1-907584-03-9) www.northstarelt.co.uk

3 Surveys

Whole class

Students carry one of the cards and then walk round the class, ask their classmates questions, keeping a note on a grid or chart of the answers.

Eg. *How do you get to school? Which is your favourite way to travel?*

After the survey, students should be ready to present the information they've collected.

4 Travel Disaster

Pairwork

Students pretend they (or a friend) have been on a trip where everything went wrong. They have to choose (or the teacher gives them) six cards at random, and the students use the prompts to tell their stories.

5 Blog/Diary

Working alone or pairwork

Ask the students to make up a blog or diary entry about a trip they have taken recently. They can talk about where they went, how they got there and if there were any problems during their trip. Ask them to give as many details as they can.

Word List: Verbs

1.	to get up	21.	to draw
2.	to get washed	22.	to love
3.	to get dressed	23.	to kiss
4.	to prepare (meal)	24.	to sit down
5.	to eat	25.	to think
6.	to drink	26.	to study
7.	to go in	27.	to refuse
8.	to go out	28.	to wait
9.	to go up	29.	to carry
10.	to go down	30.	to open
11.	to speak	31.	to look at
12.	to listen (to)	32.	to give
13.	to push	33.	to choose
14.	to pull	34.	to find
15.	to buy	35.	to meet
16.	to sell	36.	to play
17.	to arrive	37.	to run
18.	to leave	38.	to dance
19.	to read	39.	to go to bed
20.	to write	40.	to sleep

Language Games

In addition to the ideas in the section *Activities & Games for using the Mini Flashcards and Picture Pages* you can try these extra ideas for *Verbs*. See also *COPYKIT ENGLISH: Mini Flashcards Language Games Vital Verbs Teacher's Book (ISBN 978-1-907584-04-6).*

① Verbs Game

Pairwork

Use the *Verbs* cards with the cards from *People & Jobs*. Each partner has half the cards in the pack. They each take it in turns to hold up their card, and their partner has to find a verb that fits the job. If they choose a suitable verb they can keep the card.
Eg. *bank clerk = counts/takes/gives money; helps customers*

② Verb Matching Pairs

Pairwork or group work

On pieces of paper one player writes a sentence using a verb for their partner or another group to match up to the correct picture.

③ Story Time

Pairwork or Groups of 4

Students are given 10 verbs and make up a story using the verbs. The teacher can ask for suggestions beforehand for the story genre: *detective story, love story, horror story.*

© 2010 North Star ELT   **Mini Flashcards Language Games: Teacher's Book** (ISBN 978-1-907584-03-9)   www.northstarelt.co.uk

4 Routines

Pairwork

Students are given pictures which relate to routines
(Eg. to get up, to get washed, to get dressed) and have
to talk about the times they normally do these things.
Eg. *I get up at 7 a.m. and get washed after breakfast. I get
dressed at about 8 a.m. and go out at 8.30.*

5 Surveys

Whole class

Students walk round the class, ask their classmates questions about the
things they do. They should take notes about what they hear and present
the information to the class.
Eg. *What time do you usually get up? When do you leave for school?*

Word List: Weather & Calendar

1.	morning	21.	April
2.	afternoon	22.	May
3.	evening	23.	June
4.	night	24.	July
5.	day	25.	August
6.	week	26.	September
7.	month	27.	October
8.	weekend	28.	November
9.	spring	29.	December
10.	summer	30.	weather (forecast)
11.	autumn	31.	it's cold
12.	winter	32.	it's hot
13.	year	33.	it's foggy
14.	birthday	34.	it's windy
15.	Christmas	35.	it's sunny
16.	New Year's Eve	36.	the weather's bad
17.	Easter	37.	the weather's nice
18.	January	38.	it's snowing
19.	February	39.	it's freezing
20.	March	40.	it's raining

Language Games

In addition to the ideas in the section *Activities & Games for using the Mini Flashcards and Picture Pages* you can try these extra ideas for *Weather & Calendar*.

① Calendar Guessing Game

Pairwork or Groups of 3-4

Spread cards 9-12 and 18-29 out on the table. One person or group makes a sentence about a picture for other partner/group to guess.

Eg. *In this month you send Valentine's cards.*
   In this season you might see lots of snow.

② Calendar Matching Pairs

Pairwork or Group work

On pieces of paper learners write a sentence saying what happens at different times of the year for the other partner or group to match with pictures of months, seasons, or festivals.

③ Weather Matching Pairs

Pairwork or Group work

On pieces of paper learners write a sentence saying what happens in different weather conditions for the other partner or group to match to the weather cards.

Eg. *It's difficult to see. – foggy*

   © 2010 North Star ELT   **Mini Flashcards Language Games: Teacher's Book** (ISBN 978-1-907584-03-9)   www.northstarelt.co.uk

④ Weather Report

Pairwork or Group work

Provide or create large maps of the local area, your country, region or the world. Each learner has a small photocopied version of the same map and some weather forecast symbols (Eg. *sunny, snowing, raining, windy*). One player gives a weather report for the one of these maps and the others place on their maps the appropriate weather symbol. They then compare their maps to see if they are all the same.

⑤ Festivals

Pairwork

In pairs, work with cards 14-17 to talk about what the learners do at this time, or like and don't like about this festival or celebration.

Using Dice or Spinners with Mini Flashcards

Language or number dice (or spinners) can be used on their own or in combination with other dice/spinners, to add a further dimension to activities using the Mini Flashcards. Dice or spinners can also be used very effectively with the black and white photocopiable sets of pictures in this book. The dice and spinners available separately are:

6-sided dice:	(numbers 1-6)	ISBN 978-1-907584-27-5	(Spinner: 978-1-907584-63-3)
10-sided dice:	(numbers 0-9)	ISBN 978-1-907584-24-4	(Spinner: 978-1-907584-60-2)
20-sided dice:	(numbers 1-20)	ISBN 978-1-907584-26-8	(Spinner: 978-1-907584-62-6)
6-sided dice:	Colours	ISBN 978-1-907584-23-7	(Spinner: 978-1-907584-59-6)
6-sided dice:	Mood	ISBN 978-1-907584-25-1	(Spinner: 978-1-907584-61-9)
6-sided dice:	Prepositions	ISBN 978-1-907584-28-2	(Spinner: 978-1-907584-64-0)
6-sided dice:	Pronouns	ISBN 978-1-907584-29-9	(Spinner: 978-1-907584-65-7)
6-sided dice:	Questions	ISBN 978-1-907584-30-5	(Spinner: 978-1-907584-66-4)
6-sided dice:	Tenses	ISBN 978-1-907584-31-2	(Spinner: 978-1-907584-67-1)

How to make your own spinners

Alternatively, you can make spinners from the templates included in this unit. Blank spinners of different shapes and sizes are also provided for teachers to create additional prompts. If you make your own NUMBERS spinners, the numbers can be filled in sequence or at random.

Using the templates in this units, photocopy the spinners onto thin card, or photocopy onto paper and glue them onto thicker card. Make a hole in the middle, and push through a section of a relatively thick drinking straw, a (dead!) matchstick, a cocktail stick or a toothpick, or a small pencil. Secure with rubber bands or blutak around your centre on both sides of the spinner.

How to use dice or spinners with the Mini Flashcards

Here are some general suggestions for using the different dice or spinners on their own, together or with the Mini Flashcards, and the kind of language you can generate. You'll soon get ideas of your own as the possibilities are endless! You can make up your own and tailor your tasks to the language aims and level of your class.

If you have good ideas and lessons for using the dice or spinners, why not tell us and we can put your ideas on our website to share with other teachers!

Write to **english@northstarelt.co.uk**
or visit **www.northstarelt.co.uk/miniflashcards**

Question Dice/Spinner

when, why, what, how, who, where

On its Own

In the Spotlight
Players throw the dice/spinner and ask each other questions beginning with the word shown.
Eg. *Where are you? What's your name? Why are you here? How old are you? Where do you live? What's your favourite TV programme?*
You can answer truthfully or give fantasy answers.

Situation or Context Given
Eg. Excursion: *Where/when did you go? Who did you go with?*
Combined with other dice/spinner
Eg. PRONOUN dice/spinner. *When did he win Wimbledon? What do you like to eat? How does Maria get to school?*

Combined with the Mini Flashcards

Place the cards (one topic or mixed) in the middle of the table. Take a card, roll the dice, and make up a question. The next player has to answer it. One point for each correct question and answer.

Eg.   Q: *What's this?*   A: *It's a ticket.*
        Q: *Where's my ruler?*   A: *It's in your bag.*
        Q: *Who's digging in the field?*   A: *The farmer.*

Variation: A card is taken from the pack. Each player takes turns to roll the dice and ask a question about the card. Play continues until no more reasonable questions seem possible. One point per question.

Combined with Other Prompts

TV Interview
You each write down on a piece of paper the name of someone famous (or use photos of celebrities which the class brings in) fold the paper up, and put it in the middle of the table. The first player takes a paper and pretends to be that personality. The other players roll the dice and ask questions accordingly.

Pronoun Dice/Spinner

he/she, I, you, we, they, it/one

The PRONOUN dice/spinner is very useful with the *Verbs* cards.

On its Own

Make true statements about you or the people in your room as you play.
Eg. *He's my teacher. I'm hungry. He's wearing a blue shirt. They're my friends.*

Situation or Context Given
Eg. Travel: *I go to school by bus. You take the train. They walk to school.*

Combined with Other Dice

Eg. MOOD dice/spinner. *I'm fed up. They're happy. She's cross. He doesn't mind.*

Combined with the Mini Flashcards

Eg. Happy Holidays: *They're staying in a hotel. You're camping. I'm staying in a youth hostel. He's waiting for the lift.*
People & Jobs: *She's searching a suitcase. He's working on the computer.*

© 2010 North Star ELT   **Mini Flashcards Language Games: Teacher's Book** (ISBN 978-1-907584-03-9)   www.northstarelt.co.uk

Colours Dice/Spinner

red, blue, green, white, yellow, black

On its Own
Make true statements or what you can see.
Eg. *Green grass. White paper. The table is brown. My T-shirt is pink.*

Situation or Context Given
Eg. Holidays: *blue sky, blue sea, green leaves, yellow sand, white clouds*

Combined with Other Dice
NUMBERS. Eg. *10 green bottles, 2 blue eyes, 4 black tyres*
Two COLOURS dice/spinners together: *Yellow + black = a bee. Red and blue = my flag*

Combined with the Mini Flashcards
Eg. Food & Drink: *Lemons are yellow. Strawberries are red.*

Mood Dice/Spinner

This 6-sided dice/spinner is for prompting feelings, opinions, likes and dislikes.
Eg. *love, like, don't mind, don't like, really don't like, hate*
or: *very happy, happy, OK, unhappy, very unhappy, angry*

For each task you need to elicit or pre-teach the feelings or verbs which the different faces prompt. The definitions or meanings of the faces can vary from task to task, depending on the language or functions focus.

On its Own
It can be used on its own to develop learners' ability to come up with some adjectives or express feelings.
Eg. *Happy, sad, angry. I like/hate school. I don't mind Maths. I love ice-cream.*

Situation or Context Given
Eg. TV programmes: *I quite like documentaries. I hate cartoons. I love films.*

Combined with Other Dice
Eg. QUESTIONS dice/spinner: *What do you like? Why are you happy?*

Combined with the Mini Flashcards
Eg. People & Jobs: *I'd like to be a doctor. The shop assistant was really helpful. I'd hate to be a vet.*
Food & Drink: *I love strawberries. I hate apples. I don't mind eggs.*

© 2010 North Star ELT   **Mini Flashcards Language Games: Teacher's Book** (ISBN 978-1-907584-03-9)   www.northstarelt.co.uk

Tenses Dice/Spinner
> < >> <<

These prompts are based on controls you see on a DVD or a CD player:

>   (play)
>>   (fast forward)
<<   (rewind)
<   (slow rewind)

Depending on your language focus, you can choose and change the tenses that you want the dice/spinner to prompt, and pre-teach accordingly before the task.

Eg. >   SIMPLE PRESENT
     >> PRESENT CONTINUOUS
     <   PAST SIMPLE
     << PAST CONTINUOUS

or:
     >   FUTURE WITH SIMPLE PRESENT
     >> FUTURE 'WILL' or 'GOING TO'
     <   PRESENT PERFECT
     << PRESENT PERFECT CONTINUOUS

On its Own
Eg. *I get up at 7.30 a.m. The lesson finished at 3 p.m. I was playing badminton.*

Combined with Other Dice
Eg. QUESTIONS dice/spinner: *How do you come to school? When are you leaving? When did you get home?*

Combined with Mini Flashcards
Eg. Happy Holidays: *He loves camping. They've found your suitcase. He was sitting in the restaurant.*

The TENSE dice/spinner are, of course, perfect for using with the *Verbs* cards.

Prepositions Dice/Spinner
in, on, in front of, behind, next to, between

On its Own
Players throw the dice/spinner and make true statements about what they can see, using the prepositions. Eg. *I am in class. The teacher is in front of the class. Claudia is sitting next to Petra.*

Combined with Mini Flashcards
Eg. At Home: *The chair is in the kitchen. My bedroom is next to the bathroom.*
Round the Town: *The post office is next to the internet café. The car park is behind the supermarket.*

Combined with Other Prompts
Describing the Scene
Use some pictures showing some busy scenes (or maybe pictured scenes from moments in famous films), and learners use the spinner to prompt True/False statements about them. Eg. *The bus is behind the taxi. The children are next to the dog. Shrek is in the forest.*

© 2010 North Star ELT   **Mini Flashcards Language Games: Teacher's Book** (ISBN 978-1-907584-03-9)   www.northstarelt.co.uk

Numbers dice/spinner
1-6, 0-9, 1-20

On its Own
What Number Is It?
Any NUMBERS dice/spinner: In groups of 3-4, a player throws a dice/spinner and says the number. If s/he is wrong, then s/he must drop out. The last one in the game is the winner.

Telling the Time
0-9 NUMBERS dice/spinner: (in pairs or groups of 3-4, a player throws a dice/spinner and the other person or learners ask *What time is it?* and the player says *It's ___ o'clock* (0 can mean ten o'clock). If s/he is wrong, then s/he must drop out. The last one in the game is the winner. You can even adapt the spinner idea to have 24 numbers to prompt the students to say *It's 7 o'clock in the morning/a.m.* dice/spinner says 7) or *It's 10 p.m.* (dice/spinner says 22) etc.

Higher or Lower
Any dice/spinner: Throw the dice/spinner and say the number that appears. Then guess (and say out loud) if the next number thrown will be higher or lower. Then throw again. If the player is right, s/he gets a point and repeats the task. If not, it's the next player's turn.

Number Bingo
1-20 NUMBERS dice/spinner: Learners write down 8 numbers from 1-20 in words or numbers. One person throws the dice/spinner and calls out the number. The same person keeps doing this until all the numbers have been said. The first person to have all his/her numbers called is the winner.

Situation or Context Given
Eg. Prices: Roll the dice/spinner. If it is 12, for example, a player suggests something that costs *12 p, costs £1.20, costs £12.00, costs £120.00* and so on.
or:
Measurements: Suggest things that are *12 metres/miles/km long/high/wide/round/square* etc. *Weigh 12 grammes/kilos* or *Contain 12 mls/litres of (liquid)* or *Travel at 12 miles an hour*
or:
Myself: Players describe themselves.
He's 12 years old. Her birthday is the 12th. He lives at number 12 . . . It's on the 12th floor . . . I earn £12 per week. I can run 100 metres in 12 seconds. I can go round the world in 12 days.
The statements need not be true. The more outrageous, the more fun!

Combined with Other Dice
Any NUMBERS dice/spinner. Sums: Roll two dice and ask: *What's 18 + 3? What's 16 - 13?* The next player has to answer correctly to get a point.

Combined with the Mini Flashcards
Eg. Travel: *2 tickets. 3 taxis. The bus leaves at 9 a.m. The journey took 3 hours.*

Combined with Other Prompts
Eg. Supply a copy of the current Top Twenty downloaded songs or bestselling books. The players ask each other questions and give correct answers: *Which song is number 1? Who is number 6? Which book is number 15?*

My Monster
Each group throws dice or uses a spinner to prompt a description of a Monster.
Eg. *My Monster's got 7 eyes, 3 ears, 5 legs. It's 3 centimetres tall. It's 5 metres wide. My Monster's nose is 11 centimetres long.*
Each player then draws a picture of what the monster looks like. The results are then compared.

Variation: Prompt descriptions for 'Mystery Island' (*beaches, houses, people, mountains, volcanoes*) or 'Creepy Castle' (*towers, secret doors, guards, dungeons, ghosts*).

© 2010 North Star ELT   **Mini Flashcards Language Games: Teacher's Book** (ISBN 978-1-907584-03-9)   www.northstarelt.co.uk

QUESTIONS

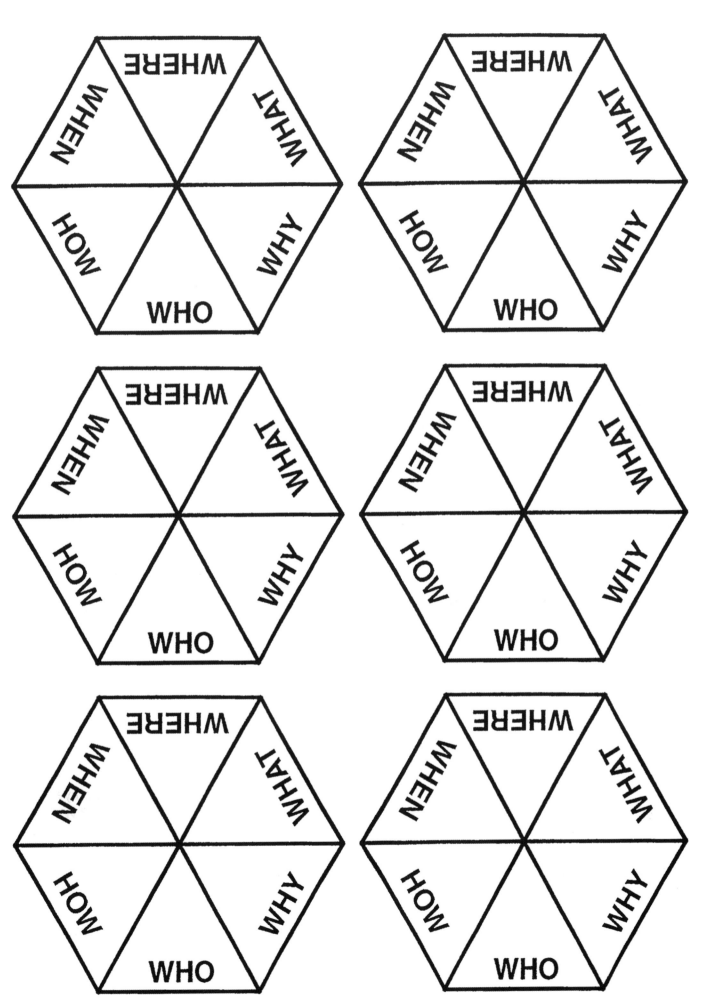

© 2010 North Star ELT   **Mini Flashcards Language Games: Teacher's Book** (ISBN 978-1-907584-03-9)   www.northstarelt.co.uk

PRONOUNS

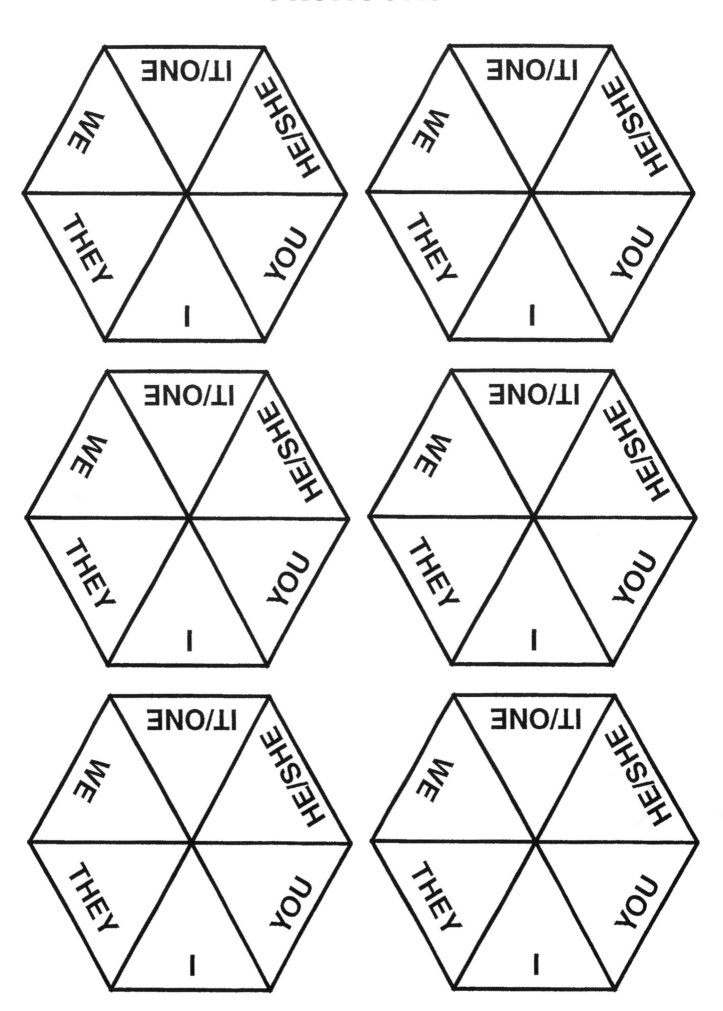

COLOURS

© 2010 North Star ELT   **Mini Flashcards Language Games: Teacher's Book** (ISBN 978-1-907584-03-9)   www.northstarelt.co.uk

MOOD

© 2010 North Star ELT   **Mini Flashcards Language Games: Teacher's Book** (ISBN 978-1-907584-03-9)   www.northstarelt.co.uk

TENSES

© 2010 North Star ELT   **Mini Flashcards Language Games: Teacher's Book** (ISBN 978-1-907584-03-9)   www.northstarelt.co.uk

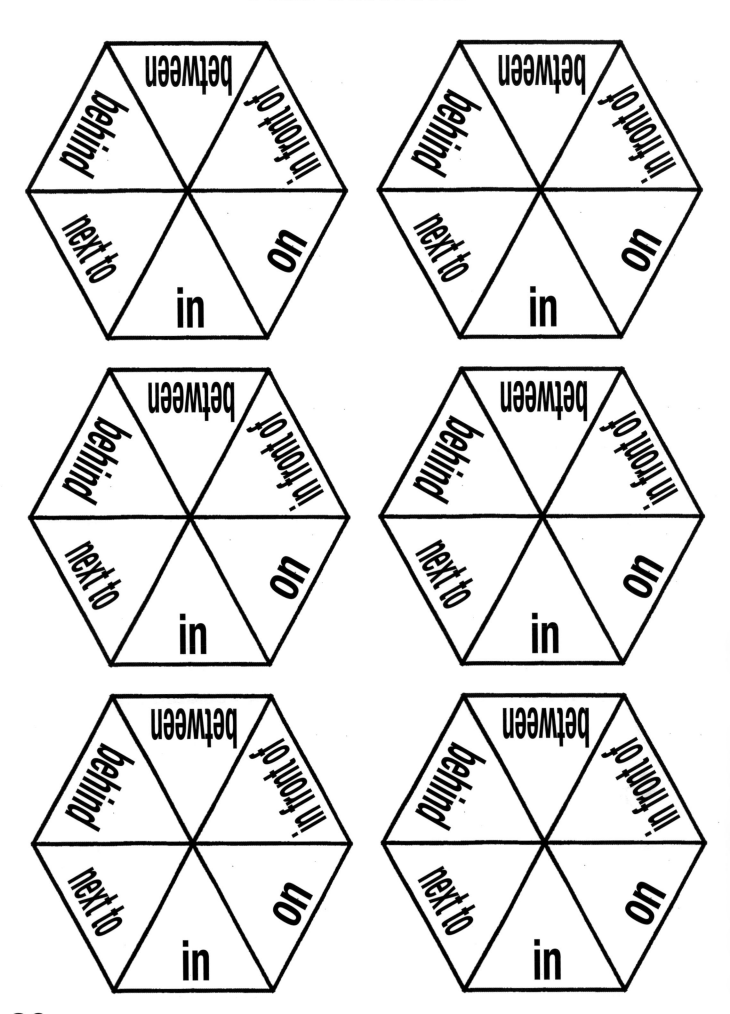

© 2010 North Star ELT   **Mini Flashcards Language Games: Teacher's Book** (ISBN 978-1-907584-03-9)   www.northstarelt.co.uk

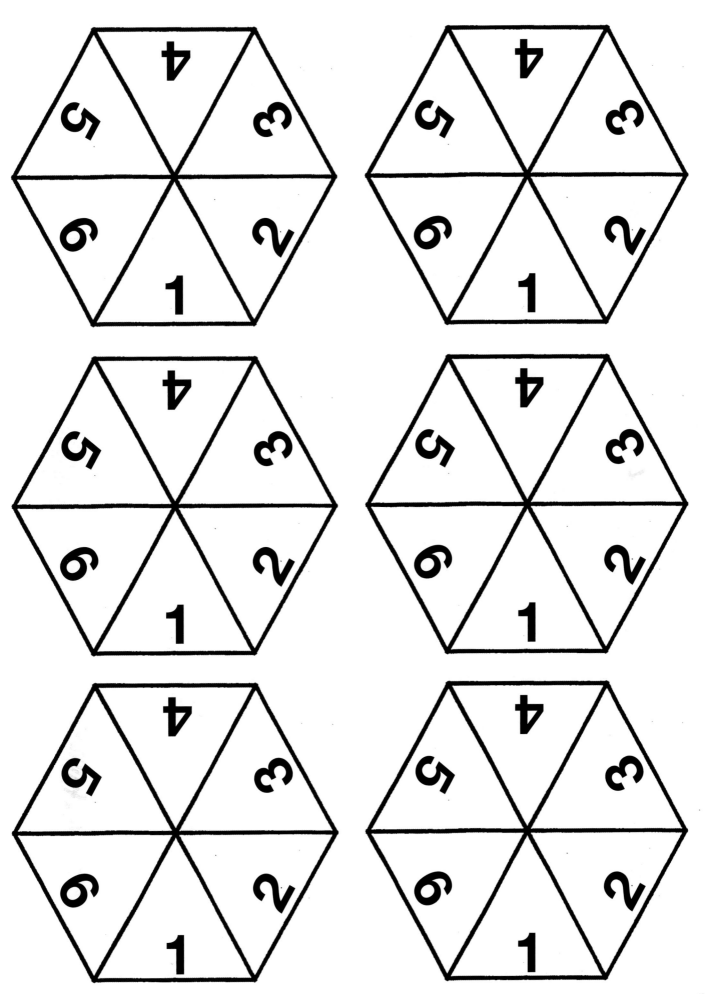

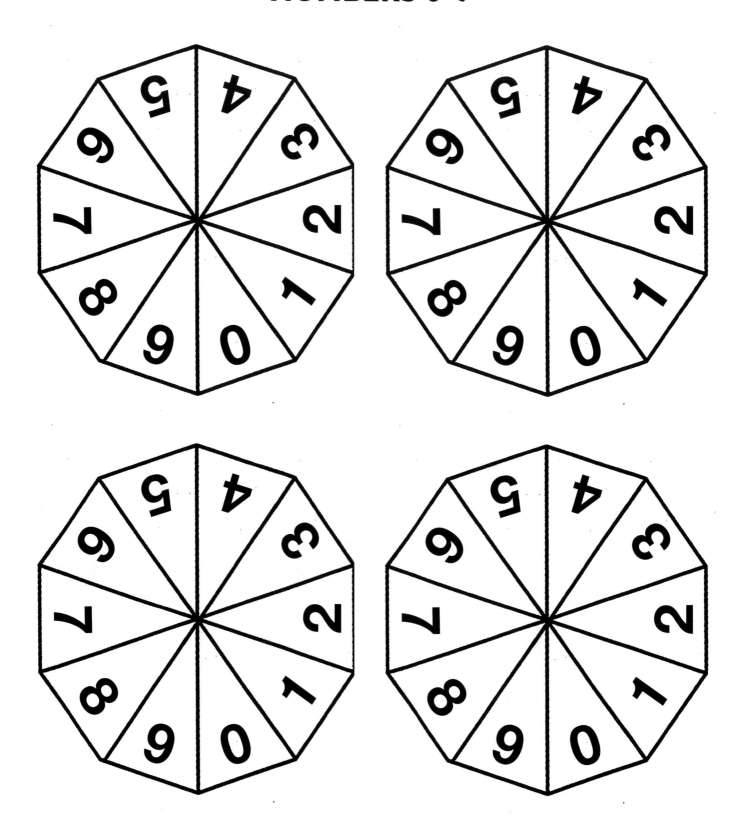

© 2010 North Star ELT **Mini Flashcards Language Games: Teacher's Book** (ISBN 978-1-907584-03-9) www.northstarelt.co.uk

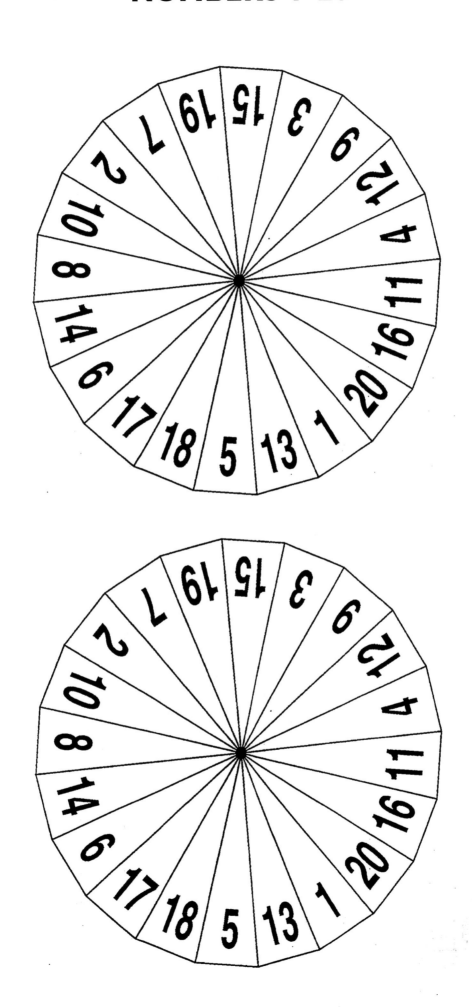

Mixing and Matching the Mini Flashcards

The resources can be used in a variety of combinations. This chart shows some of the obvious combinations which have been used successfully. Combinations refer either to full packs of cards or selected cards.

	Food	Leisure	Travel	Weather	Jobs	Verbs	Hols.	Town	Body	Clothes	Adj.	Preps.	Home	School	Feelings	Me	Number	Colour	Mood	Tense	Tense 2	Questions	Pronoun
Pronoun	✓	✓		✓	✓	✓			✓							✓			✓	✓	✓	✓	
Questions	✓	✓	✓	✓	✓	✓	✓	✓	✓		✓	✓	✓			✓	✓						✓
Tense 2																							
Tense	✓	✓	✓	✓	✓	✓	✓	✓	✓				✓	✓			✓			✓	✓		
Mood	✓	✓	✓	✓		✓	✓		✓			✓	✓					✓		✓	✓		
Colour	✓												✓					✓					
Number	✓	✓			✓		✓					✓	✓			✓							
Me		✓			✓														✓		✓	✓	
Feelings	✓	✓	✓			✓	✓		✓			✓	✓						✓		✓		
School								✓	✓			✓		✓	✓	✓	✓		✓				
Home								✓	✓				✓	✓	✓	✓	✓		✓				
Preps.		✓				✓					✓	✓						✓					
Adj.	✓	✓	✓	✓		✓	✓		✓			✓						✓		✓			
Clothes		✓		✓	✓			✓		✓			✓		✓	✓	✓	✓		✓		✓	✓
Body		✓			✓				✓									✓					
Town			✓				✓	✓		✓						✓	✓		✓	✓		✓	✓
Hols.									✓			✓		✓		✓	✓		✓	✓			
Verbs				✓			✓													✓	✓	✓	
Jobs					✓	✓		✓	✓				✓	✓	✓	✓	✓	✓	✓				
Weather	✓	✓					✓						✓					✓		✓			
Travel			✓					✓	✓				✓		✓		✓	✓	✓	✓	✓		
Leisure			✓										✓		✓		✓		✓			✓	✓
Food										✓			✓		✓	✓	✓	✓					

Mini Flashcards Language Games: Teacher's Book (ISBN 978-1-907584-03-9) www.northstarelt.co.uk

Using Function Cards

Many language programmes and coursebooks are organised around topics. While this has many advantages for the learner, teachers sometimes find that learners tend to associate certain vocabulary and structures with certain topics, and need to be given opportunities to discover how language they have already learned can be used in quite different situations. If learners are to develop fluency in the language, they must be aware, right from the beginning, that a little language can go a long way.

Using the Mini Flashcards together with Function Cards, learners can be provided with 'risk-free' situations in which to engage experimentally in the use of known language in new, and perhaps unfamiliar, contexts. In so doing, they will build up confidence in their ability to cope with the unpredictability of language in real life contexts.

The sample Function Cards shown below illustrate the potential of such an approach.

Using Function Cards

Example 1
Prepare a card with the instruction:

Ask for information

Select a set of Mini Flashcards or visuals which show different situations in which a learner might want to *ask for information*. For example, you could use cards from *Leisure, Travel, People & Jobs, Verbs, Happy Holidays, Round the Town*.

Example 2
Prepare a card with the instruction:

Make a request
or
Ask for help

Select a set of cards or visuals which show different situations in which a learner might want to *make a request or ask for help*. For example, you could use cards from *Leisure, Travel, Weather & Calendar, People & Jobs, Happy Holidays, Round the Town*.

You can create a large, varied pile of Function Cards to reflect and develop situations in the topics you are (or have been) working on, for use with Mini Flashcards — or for practice in new situations. Hundreds of ideas are possible using just a few cards.

Function Cards can be used at any level, provided that learners understand that there are various ways of saying the same thing, and that what is important is to get the message across. For example: if the learner has cards which require her/him to ask for information about the hospital, and has decided to ask for directions, he/she could say:
Hospital, please?
Where's the hospital?
Excuse me, can you tell me where the hospital is? etc.
Each student can therefore use language at his/her own level.

Once learners have got the idea that language is transferable from one situation to another, the teacher might, when introducing a new topic, explore with the class which functions might apply to the new situation and what language they already have at their disposal.

As your learners get used to activities using Function Cards, you might prefer to start off with Function Cards instructions in their first language. Later on, instructions can be printed in English.

Using Function Cards to Encourage Learners to Say More

In the examples above, single Function Cards are used with a range of pictures depicting situations. Another way to use Function Cards is to provide a number of them with one suitable picture only, and to ask the learner to use the ideas thus generated to say as much as they can either about the picture or imagining they are in the picture.

Example 1

With the picture *In Hospital* (from *Round the Town*) the learner(s) could be asked to produce language matching any of the following suggested Function Cards:

Say what this is	*Make a comparison*
Say what usually happens here	*Mention something you like*
Describe something	*Mention something you don't like*
Request something	*Say how you feel about it*
Give instructions	*Make a wish*

Once ideas have been generated, learners could be asked to give a talk or write a piece about a visit to the hospital, doctor or dentist. The same set of Function Cards could be used with other locations.

Example 2

Using the picture *At a Party* (from *Leisure*), prepare a selection of Function Cards along the following lines:

Ask for/give information	*Make an appointment*
Describe what someone's doing	*Ask for/state a preference*
Make/reply to a request	*Report an event in the past*
Give some instructions	*Ask for/give permission to do something*
Give/accept an invitation	*Persuade someone to do something.*

After brainstorming this situation, learners could be asked to write a dialogue or perform a short scene.

Activities and Games Using Function Cards

- Many of the activities and games already described can be adapted for use with Function Cards.
- Pages of the visuals can be photocopied for use in this way, with players throwing a suitably numbered dice to select the situation for which they are to provide the language item shown on the Function Card.
- Sequences of Function Cards can be used to prompt the composition of dialogues.

© 2010 North Star ELT   **Mini Flashcards Language Games: Teacher's Book** (ISBN 978-1-907584-03-9)   www.northstarelt.co.uk

MINI FLASHCARDS LANGUAGE GAMES
FUNCTION CARDS

Say what this is	Say what usually happens here	Describe something	Request something
Give instructions	Make a comparison	Mention something you like	Mention something you don't like
Say how you feel about it	Make a wish	Ask for/give information	Describe what someone's doing
Make/reply to a request	Give some instructions	Give/accept an invitation	Make an appointment
Ask for/state a preference	Report an event in the past	Ask for/give permission to do something	Persuade someone to do something

© 2010 North Star ELT   **Mini Flashcards Language Games: Teacher's Book** (ISBN 978-1-907584-03-9)   www.northstarelt.co.uk

MINI FLASHCARDS LANGUAGE GAMES
FUNCTION CARDS TEMPLATE

© 2010 North Star ELT   **Mini Flashcards Language Games: Teacher's Book** (ISBN 978-1-907584-03-9)   www.northstarelt.co.uk

MINI FLASHCARDS TEMPLATE

1	2	3	4
5	6	7	8
9	10	11	12
13	14	15	16
17	18	19	20

Mini Flashcards Language Games: Teacher's Book (ISBN 978-1-907584-03-9)   www.northstarelt.co.uk

MINI FLASHCARDS TEMPLATE

21	22	23	24
25	26	27	28
29	30	31	32
33	34	35	36
37	38	39	40

© 2010 North Star ELT   **Mini Flashcards Language Games: Teacher's Book** (ISBN 978-1-907584-03-9)   www.northstarelt.co.uk

MINI FLASHCARDS TEMPLATE

1	2	3
4	5	6
7	8	9
10	11	12